LANGSTON HUGHES

BONNIE GREER was born on the Southside of Chicago. She has lived in the United Kingdom for many years, and is both an American and British citizen. She is an award-winning playwright and novelist, as well as an author, critic and broadcaster. She has taught playwriting in schools in both New York City and in London. She was awarded an OBE for services to the arts in the Queen's Birthday Honours in 2010.

LANGSTON HUGHES

The Value of Contradiction

BONNIE GREER

Arcadia Books Ltd
15–16 Nassau Street
London W1W 7AB

www.arcadiabooks.com

First published by BlackAmber Inspirations,
an imprint of Arcadia Books 2011

A catalogue record for this book is available from the British Library.

ISBN 978-1-906413-76-7

Typeset in Minion by MacGuru Ltd
Printed and bound in the United Kingdom by CPI Cox & Wyman, Reading, RG1 8EX

Arcadia Books gratefully acknowledges the financial support of Arts Council England.

Arcadia Books supports PEN, the fellowship of writers who work together to promote
literature and its understanding. English PEN upholds writers' freedoms in Britain and
around the world, challenging political and cultural limits on free expression.
To find out more, visit *www.englishpen.org* or contact
English PEN, Free Word Centre, 60 Farringdon Road, London EC1R 3GA

Arcadia Books distributors are as follows:

in the UK and elsewhere in Europe:
Turnaround Publishers Services
Unit 3, Olympia Trading Estate
Coburg Road
London N22 6TZ

in the USA and Canada:
Dufour Editions
PO Box 7
Chester Springs
PA, 19425

in Australia:
The GHR Press
PO Box 7109
McMahons Point
Sydney 2060

in New Zealand:
Addenda
Box 78224
Grey Lynn
Auckland

in South Africa:
Jacana Media (Pty) Ltd
PO Box 291784
Melville 2109 6Johannesburg

Arcadia Books is the *Sunday Times* Small Publisher of the Year

For my brother the poet/educator Ben Greer III and our great-nephew, Cameron Jay Greer

Contents

PROLOGUE

'Langston Hughes Tells Senators He's Against Communists.'

AFRICAN AMERICAN READERS opening their 9 April 1953 edition of the black tabloid magazine *Jet* would have been surprised to see this caption anywhere near a photo of the man widely considered to be the poet laureate of African America. Langston Hughes was considered the champion of his people, an inspiration for people of African descent all over the world, for all oppressed peoples, no matter what colour they were.

He had written hundreds of poems, numerous novels, works for children, dozens of short stories, plays, essays, operas, screenplays, autobiographies, had taught at numerous universities. His matrix was the African American experience, with all of its beauty and passion, humour, fearlessness and, above all, truth. In photos of Langston at the Senate hearing, he looks almost apologetic, accommodating, as if he is trying to bring his hostile interrogators over to his side.

His immortal creation, a black Everyman, a man who spoke in the voice of ordinary black people – 'Jesse B. Semple', known as 'Simple' – would have mocked Langston mercilessly. 'Hypocrite' would have been the least of Simple's terms to describe Langston, sitting at the table of his enemies, appearing as a 'friendly witness' before Joseph McCarthy's notorious Senate Permanent Subcommittee on Investigations. Simple would have said that Langston Hughes was trying to be nice to a group of politicians not worthy to tie his shoelaces.

Unfortunately, what the readers of *Jet* would have seen was this: one of the role models of the black community had sold out. Bowed down. Gave 'them' everything they wanted. Langston Hughes had become a witness.

There were two types of witness: 'hostile' – those who appeared but who did not speak, invoking the Fifth Amendment of the US Constitution which gives citizens the right not to incriminate themselves; or those who answered questions but not with the answers the Committee wanted. And then there were the 'friendly' witnesses who cooperated.

Langston cooperated.

Everyone in America knew that the Committee existed to expose what it considered to be 'enemies' of America. Those enemies were usually on the Left. Appearing as a friendly witness was not only about giving individual personal testimony, it could open a floodgate that could destroy friends and associates as well. Langston knew this. Because of who he was and what his life and work had stood for, Langston would have been expected by one and all to be a hostile witness. He didn't even have to show up.

Charlie Chaplin hadn't.

Charlie had been the biggest movie star on the planet when Langston was a child, a huge cultural force. Charlie had refused to appear when subpoenaed, and instead had taken his young American family first to his native London, and finally to Switzerland. He returned briefly about twenty years later to accept a special Oscar and then left again.

Or, if Langston had decided to appear, he could have refused to answer questions, like the black professor Doxey A. Wilkerson had done earlier on the very same day that Langston had appeared. Being a great poet, Langston could have said something elegant when questioned, like the screenwriter John Howard Lawson had done a few years before:

Questioner: 'Are you now or have you ever been a member of the Communist Party of the United States?'

Lawson: 'It's unfortunate and tragic that I have to teach this committee the basic principles of Americanism … I shall continue to fight for the Bill of Rights, which you are trying to destroy.'

By being before the Senate, it seemed to many that Langston was repudiating everything he had once stood for, turning his back on it all on that spring day on Capitol Hill, Washington DC. Langston was quoted in *Jet* as saying to the Committee that he was 'amazed' to learn that his old pro-Communist writings were in State Department libraries abroad. This was the 'reason' the Committee had given for summoning him

But Langston assured them that since 'race relations had improved' in the US, America was a better place than the Soviet Union. The average black person would have been shocked by this reply. Unfortunately many young black people, particularly artists, would not have been shocked. This generation, veterans of World War II, were vocal and standing up for their rights, in housing and jobs, in the courts and in the streets. To them Langston was old-fashioned. To others, by going to the Senate, he was a traitor to the Cause.

And they cast him out of their minds and their hearts.

Decades after his appearance before that Senate

Subcommittee, Langston Hughes has been elevated to that pantheon of African American and African Caribbean writers who make up the golden age of the Harlem Renaissance. He is now considered one of the Renaissance's leading lights, a visionary, an African American man determined to have a literary career, and to have it in America.

Langston Hughes was a handsome, cultured man of small stature, a man who took Walt Whitman, the nineteenth-century poet who had changed American poetry forever, as one of his role models. But it was to black working-class people that Langston looked for inspiration. It was they whom he celebrated.

Langston has been called the 'Father of Black Consciousness', the leading African American writer of the last century. There are many interpretations of his life, aspects of which are still being discovered because his output was prodigious and varied. Some of it is still coming to light. This is what is known:

Between the ages of twenty-seven and twenty-eight, Langston published his first novel *Not Without Laughter* which won the prestigious 1931 Harmon Gold Medal for Literature. His first collection of short stories was published four years later. Both of these works were literary breakthroughs in the creation of the style known as social realism. In 1935, when he was in his early thirties, Langston received a Guggenheim Fellowship; in 1938, he established the Harlem

Suitcase Theater in New York City; a year later, the New Negro Theater in Los Angeles; and two years after that, the Skyloft Players in Chicago. He was energetic and prolific.

But racism, its relentless grind, was always present. He found it everywhere.

The year that Langston opened the New Negro Theater in Los Angeles, he wrote a screenplay. By then he was a successful Broadway playwright who wanted to try his hand at the movies. But Hollywood had no place for a black screenwriter and only the most restricted of places for black on-screen talent. For example, when Hattie McDaniel won her Oscar for Best Supporting Actress for *Gone With The Wind*, she had to enter through the kitchen entrance of the restaurant where the award ceremony was being held. Black people could not enter through the front door.

The immortal Queen of Jazz, the vocalist Ella Fitzgerald, was originally considered for the part of 'Sam', Humphrey Bogart's sidekick in the classic film *Casablanca*. But it would have been impossible to cast a black woman in a role opposite a white male leading actor which could have implied a relationship with romantic and/or sexual overtones. Any movie theatre showing a film like that would have been in serious danger. So 'Sam' became an African American man, rather than an African American woman.

During World War II the African American singer and actress Lena Horne, a universally acknowledged beauty, was signed by the mega-studio MGM in part to placate the black troops fighting abroad who had no 'glamour girl' of their own in the movies. But Lena's magnificent beauty and voice were too often showcased in a solitary environment within the film. This made it easier to cut her part for the segregated movies houses in the Deep South.

Like so many others, Langston suffered because of this suppression of his art. Who knows what he and others could have contributed to the culture of film if they had been free to participate.

It was the Communist Party USA (CPUSA) that was ready and willing to fight against racism. All African Americans were aware of this. To have been associated with the Communist Party or its affiliates, particularly during the Great Depression of the 1930s when millions suffered, would make perfect sense. During the war the Soviet Union was an ally of the United States. But afterwards, the two superpowers squared up to one another and the cold war had begun. The Soviet Union was seen as the new enemy, and its ideology – communism – in the minds and hearts of many Americans, became the United States' biggest threat.

It was Langston's past association with communism and socialism that had led him before the

Senate hearing, an association shared with many Americans. The Communist Party was never outlawed – this would have been unconstitutional. But from the late 1940s to the mid 1950s, anyone who was a member of the Party, associated with Party members, who sympathised with communism and/or socialism (a 'fellow traveller'), or was believed to have been involved with 'un-American' activities, could be called before two committees of the United States Congress. The House of Representatives' (the lower house of Congress) committee was called the House Un-American Activities Committee (HUAC) and that is the name that most people give to both it and its counterpart in the upper chamber, the Senate.

Langston was called to testify before both committees over a period of a few years in the late 1940s and early 1950s. These hearings were one form of anti-communist hysteria, a hysteria which took many forms. Other forms were the 'Blacklist' and a publication called *Red Channels*.

The Hollywood Blacklist was a secret 'pact' among employers, journalists, some members of Congress, the police and the military, that prevented suspected communists and 'fellow travellers' from making a livelihood, sometimes with tragic consequences. *Red Channels* was a magazine that named suspected show-business personalities as past or present members of the Communist Party as well as fellow

travellers. Being named in R... [handwritten note obscures text]
listing. Career extinction.

Langston Hughes was bot... [obscured]
and of *Red Channels*. The pr... [obscured]
mous. While never a comm... [obscured]
had not been hesitant in tur... [obscured]
of the oppressed and he worl... [obscured]
organisation dedicated to do... [obscured]

One of his poems, 'Goodbye, Christ' had begun
the witch-hunt that had brought him before the Senate. It was published in a left-leaning journal called
the *Negro Worker* in the early 1930s.

> *Goodbye,*
> *Christ Jesus Lord God Jehova,*
> *Beat it on away from here now.*
> *Make way for a new guy with no religion at all—*
> *A real guy named*
> *Marx Communist Lenin Peasant Stalin Worker ME—*
> *I said, ME!*

Through this poem he had made a mortal enemy
of the most powerful and charismatic evangelist of
the age, the Sarah Palin of her time, Aimee Semple
McPherson.

On a spring day in 1953, Langston, eager to get on
with his work, to go back to his poetry, appears

[Handwritten note on affixed paper:] (fellow Traveler) Langston H. denies God due to injustice and fights as he was blacklist from Communist.

before the Senate. He has even allowed Joseph McCarthy's notorious and sinister assistant, Roy Cohn, to coach him in preparation for the big day. He makes his testimony. Afterwards, this great champion of the poor, of the dispossessed, of his people, walks out of the chamber.

It is on this April day in Washington, in 1953, in front of the world, that Langston shows his willingness to defend the true Cause of his life. It was his ancestors, the Langston Family, who had paved the way for him to have the strength to do this.

To understand Langston Hughes, it is necessary to know these remarkable people.

CHAPTER ONE

'YOU SEE, UNFORTUNATELY, I am not black. There are lots of different kinds of blood in our family … "Negro" is used to mean anyone who has any Negro blood at all in his veins. In Africa, the word is more pure. It means all Negro, therefore black. I am brown. My father was a darker brown. My mother an olive-yellow. On my father's side, the white blood in his family came from a Jewish slave trader in Kentucky, Silas Cushenberry, of Clark County, who was his mother's father; and Sam Clay, a distiller of Scotch descent, living in Henry County, who was his father's father. So on my father's side both male great-grandparents were white, and Sam Clay was said to be a relative of the great statesman, Henry Clay, his contemporary. On my mother's side, I had a paternal great-grandfather named Quarles – Captain Ralph Quarles – who was white and lived in Louisa County, Virginia, before the Civil War … The Quarleses traced their ancestry back to Francis

Quarles, famous Jacobean poet, who wrote "A Feast for Wormes'".*

Langston wrote this about both sides of his family, but it was the maternal side, the Langstons, who were to have the most impact on his life and on the history of America at large. Through them Langston was the heir to a powerful legacy. This legacy began in the state of Virginia.

The first known Africans in British North America (the United States and Canada) arrived in Virginia (named after the 'Virgin Queen' Elizabeth I) in 1619. These Africans were not technically enslaved, although they had been captured on their way to slavery by English pirates. The pirates, on releasing them, enabled them to become not slaves but indentured servants, people who sold their labour for a period of time. The majority of English settlers were *also* indentured servants. The Africans, however, proved to be hardier than their English counterparts and better at survival.

By the 1640s and 50s, many Africans had worked off their indentureship, enabling them to own land, and, in time, make families with other Africans, as

* This is an edited extract from Langston Hughes' *The Big Sea*, published by the University of Missouri Press as Volume 13 of its *Collected Works of Langston Hughes* © The Estate of Langston Hughes.

well as with English and indigenous peoples. The false idea of black people in the South always having lived in slavery stems largely from the reality of black Southern life in the 1700s, not before. It was before the eighteenth century that black churches thrived in both the North and the South, part of the 'Great Awakening', a religious revival that came into being through open-air preaching, revival meetings, and the reading, by ministers, of dense, complex and emotional sermons. America has always been a nation of powerful churches and strong religious feeling. Aligned with and out of this would often come political movements. For example, some parts of the Tea Party Movement in America have a strong Evangelical Christian base.

The Civil Rights Movement of the 1950s and 60s was rooted in the Baptist and African Methodist Episcopal churches. Martin Luther King himself was a minister.

The sermons of the 'Great Awakening', their delivery and ideas, led in Britain to the ending of the slave trade on the high seas, and in America to the War of Independence. By 1775, the year before the American Revolutionary War broke out, Africans made up twenty per cent of the population, the second largest ethnic group after the English. Africans, both enslaved and free, took up arms when they could. One of them, Crispus Attucks, probably also half

Native American, is known as the first martyr for American freedom. He was killed during an altercation with British soldiers, known as the Boston Massacre, on 5 March 1770, the date that marks the beginning of the American Revolution.*

And many American patriots who fought in the Revolution came from the state of Virginia. The great American Revolutionary War orator Patrick Henry was a Virginian, prominent in Louisa County, Virginia. His name is on a plaque there along with the names of two other famous people of the town, sons of Virginia: Charles Henry Langston (1817–1892), and John Mercer Langston (1829–1897), the grandfather and great-uncle of Langston Hughes.

The Langston brothers were from a most unusual family. They were black children and along with their older brother Gideon, they were born free, at a time when most black children born in America were not born free. Their father, a white plantation owner, chose to have a family life with their mother. A quite audacious act.

On a date unknown, Ralph Quarles became involved with a woman of African and Native American descent by the name of Lucy Jane Langston. Some

---

* Martin Luther King Jr refers to Crispus Attucks in the introduction to *Why We Can't Wait* (1964). The first line of the Stevie Wonder song 'Black Man' is about him.

4

say that Lucy was enslaved and Ralph accepted her as collateral for a debt. When the debtor defaulted, Ralph legally owned Lucy. Others say that Lucy was a freedwoman, not enslaved. What is not in doubt is that Lucy and Ralph had a daughter they called Maria. Because it was against the law at that time for a white person and a person of African descent to marry (miscegenation) Maria had to take her mother's name: Langston. Ralph and Lucy had a further three children, all sons. Gideon, the oldest, looked so much like his father that he took his last name and was known as Gideon Quarles. Charles Henry was the middle son and John Mercer the youngest. John Mercer, the baby of the family, had an amazing life.

He took a bachelor's degree in 1849 and a master's degree in theology in 1852 from Oberlin College. Denied admission to law schools in New York and Ohio because he was black, he went on instead to study law with Philemon Bliss, one of the most famous lawyers of the time, and after completing his studies, he tried again and was admitted to the Ohio Bar in 1854. In the same year he married Caroline Matilda Wall who had also graduated from Oberlin College. She was the freed daughter of an enslaved mother and a wealthy white planter, Colonel Stephen Wall. Wall had freed his children and sent Caroline and her sister to Ohio for an education. Caroline, a bright and beautiful woman, met her match in John

Mercer, married him, and together they had five children.

In 1863, during the American Civil War, the government approved the founding of the United States Colored Troops and John Mercer was appointed to recruit black Americans to fight on the Union side. He enlisted hundreds of men for duty in the Massachusetts 54th and 55th as well as 800 men for Ohio's first black regiment. After the war, John Mercer worked tirelessly to ensure the vote for black men (women could not vote) and helped set up the National Equal Rights League, a precursor of the National Association for the Advancement of Colored People (NAACP), the black civil rights organisation which is still going strong in the United States today.

In 1868 John Mercer moved to Washington DC to establish and serve as dean of Howard University, the first black law school in the country. He was also the first president of Virginia Normal and Collegiate Institute, a black college at Petersburg, Virginia. President Ulysses S. Grant appointed him a member of the Board of Health of the District of Columbia. And in 1877 President Hayes appointed John Mercer US Minister to Haiti; later he became chargé d'affaires to the Dominican Republic.

In 1888, after a contested election, John Mercer took his seat in the US Congress. He was the only black person to do so from Virginia until the election of Robert Cortez 'Bobby' Scott for the 3rd congressional district of Virginia ... in 1993. Congressman Scott is, incidentally, the first Filipino to serve as a voting member of Congress because his maternal grandfather was of Filipino descent. John Mercer Langston's legacy is profound. His house in Oberlin, Ohio is a national monument; Langston University in Oklahoma is named after him; several university halls bear his name; there is even a golf course named after him in Washington. And his niece, Charles Henry's daughter, named her second child after him: James Mercer Langston Hughes. This is Langston Hughes' full name.

John Mercer had an incredible life for a little black boy who had lost his parents at the age of four and had to start a new life in another state with his older brothers and half-brother, William Langston. Thanks to a substantial legacy from their father, John Mercer and his brothers were able to be taken out of Virginia and upriver to the North, to the state of Ohio, a much safer environment for black people. Little black boys, even in the North, could be sold 'down river' into slavery in the Deep South. This is the origin of the expression 'to be sold down river' – i.e. being relegated to a dire fate.

The Langston brothers and their half-brother ended up in the town of Chillicothe in Ohio, where little John Mercer was taken to live with William

Gooch and his family, friends of his father, and his older brother Charles Henry went to school. Charles Henry, too, graduated from Oberlin College.

Oberlin College has a special place in African American history. It was the first American institution of higher learning to regularly admit black male and female students, giving it the double distinction of being co-ed and racially integrated at a time when neither black people nor women were routinely given access to higher education. Among Oberlin's future distinguished graduates was John Langalibalele Dube, first President of the African National Congress in South Africa. Mary Jane Patterson, the maternal grandmother of Langston Hughes, graduated from Oberlin in 1862, the first African American woman to earn a B.A. degree.

Both the college and the town of Oberlin were founded in 1833 by a pair of Presbyterian ministers. The college attained prominence because of the influence of its second president, the evangelist Charles Finney, one of the co-founders of the Ohio Anti-Slavery Society in April 1835. This organisation was to play a big part in the lives of the Langston brothers.

Oberlin College, and the town of Oberlin, made no secret of the fact that it was vehemently, even violently, opposed to the slave trade. Both the town and the college offered aid and comfort to escaped slaves and those who supported them. By the 1850s, the nation had become a bubbling cauldron of hate with the violent dispute over slavery at the heart of it. The dispute over slavery laid bare the real issue: which was sovereign, the federal government or the individual state? This is an argument which still lies at the heart of American political life today.

Slavery, which underpinned the entire economic, political and social system of the South brought into relief the question of whether the United States could stay united. This question began to reach breaking point by the 1850s. Any territory that wanted to become a part of the Union had to decide whether it would enter as a 'slave' state or a 'free' state.

This decision was sometimes not left to the vote.

Rather it was left to the gun.

The South hoped that Kansas would enter the Union as a slave state. Those opposed to slavery in Kansas set up their own shadow government. The term 'bushwacker' – a man who rides out of the woods to attack – comes from Kansas, a state full of secret militias, secret societies, outlaws and range riders fighting each other to the death. 'Bleeding Kansas' was one part of the mix that went into creating the time bomb that was the US in the 1850s.

New England abolitionists formed the Emigrant Aid Company to send anti-slavery settlers to the territory. Pro-slavery adherents there prepared for what they termed an invasion. 'We are threatened,' someone complained in a letter, 'with being made the unwilling receptacle of the filth, scum and offscourings of the East … to preach abolition and dig Underground Railroads.'

The letter-writer had reason to fear.

The Underground Railroad was an informal network of secret routes and safe houses, much like the system that the French Resistance set up during World War II. It was created by abolitionists and free black people and was 'conducted', at great risk, by plantation escapees like the immortal Harriet Tubman. Free black people were at risk, too, because if healthy and of reproductive age, they were considered eligible for enslavement. The Fugitive Slave Act of 1850 allowed any white person to arrest any black person suspected of being a runaway slave. People could be kidnapped and sent 'down river', never to be heard from again.

This is why the Underground Railroad was crucial. The Railroad had its own culture. People who helped the enslaved locate the Railroad were 'agents' or 'shepherds'. Guides were 'conductors'; hiding places 'stations'; 'stationmasters' hid slaves in their own homes; escapee slaves were 'passengers' or 'cargo'. The people who financed the system were 'stockholders'. The gospel song 'Follow The Drinkin' Gourd', used on the Underground Railroad, was a 'code' song. It referred to the North Star, the Big Dipper, the constellation that points to True North. Oberlin, Ohio was a station on the Underground Railroad as were: Boston, Massachusetts; Chicago, Illinois, Philadelphia, Pennsylvania, and Windsor, Ontario.

Kansas and the Underground Railroad were two of the matches that lit the flame of the Civil War.

And the Dred Scott case was another.

Dred Scott was born into slavery in Virginia. He was allowed to marry because the woman he wanted to marry, also enslaved, was sold to Dred's master. Dred lived and worked in free states for his master, and when his master returned to a slave state, Dred and his wife accompanied him. When his owner died, Dred asked to be freed, because he and his wife had lived in a free state, where slavery had been outlawed. The widow of his former owner refused to free him and Dred Scott took his case to court. The Supreme Court, in 1858, ruled that Dred had no case because he was property and property is protected under the Fifth Amendment to the Constitution. In other words, people of African descent were not human beings and therefore had no recourse to the law. This left every black person open to kidnapping and worse. Dred and his wife were sent back 'down river', but were freed by his new owner, an abolitionist. The most famous enslaved person in America at the time, Dred Scott only lived seventeen months after he was freed.

The stress and strain of it all had taken its toll.

The stress and strain of it all had also pushed the Langston brothers to breaking point. In addition to working for the Underground Railroad itself, the brothers helped lead the Ohio Anti-Slavery Society. John Mercer was president, Charles Henry was executive secretary. It was an escaped slave who would put their ideals and their courage to the test.

John Price had escaped slavery in Kentucky and had made his way to Ohio. On 13 September 1858 he was arrested by a United States marshal in Oberlin. The marshal was well aware of Oberlin's reputation so, in order to avoid any trouble, the marshal moved John Price to another town, Columbus. En route to the slaveholder's plantation in Kentucky, the marshal took John Price to the railroad station at Wellington, Ohio. A group of Oberlin residents found out and rushed to Wellington. There they joined Wellington abolitionists and attempted to free John Price. The marshal and his deputies took refuge in a hotel. Peaceful negotiations to free him failed. The rescuers invaded the hotel and took him to Oberlin to hide him. Not long after that, they set him on the route of the Underground Railroad through which he eventually reached Canada. In Canada, since the British had abolished slavery there in 1830, John Price did not have to worry. He was in another country and out of US federal control.

But this was not the end of the matter.

The 'Oberlin-Wellington Rescue', as it came to be called, became famous and caused a huge uproar. A federal grand jury brought indictments against thirty-seven of those who freed John Price. Two of the thirty-seven were the Langston brothers. But two men were sent for trial: a white abolitionist and Charles Henry Langston. Four prominent local attorneys took the case for the defence. The jury convicted the white abolitionist. They then turned to Charles Henry. His lawyers argued that the jury could not be impartial. Charles Henry was not only a known and active fighter for black freedom, he was also a black fighter for black freedom.

Charles Henry made a rousing speech defending his actions: '... But I stand up here to say, that if for doing what I did on that day at Wellington, I am to go to jail six months, and pay a fine of a thousand dollars, according to the Fugitive Slave Law, and such is the protection the laws of this country afford me, I must take upon my self the responsibility of self-protection; and when I come to be claimed by some perjured wretch as his slave, I shall never be taken into slavery. And as in that trying hour I would have others do to me, as I would call upon my friends to help me; as I would call upon you, your Honour, to help me; as I would call upon you [to the District Attorney] to help me; and upon you [to Judge Bliss], and upon

13

you [to his counsel], so help me GOD! I stand here to say that I will do all I can, for any man thus seized and help, though the inevitable penalty of six months' imprisonment and one thousand dollars fine for each offence hangs over me! We have a common humanity. You would do so; your manhood would require it; and no matter what the laws might be, you would honour yourself for doing it; your friends would honour you for doing it; your children to all generations would honour you for doing it; and every good and honest man would say, you had done right!"*

Charles Henry received twenty days in jail, a light sentence.

He and his fellow abolitionist filed a writ of habeas corpus (a writ which would have immediately released them from jail) with the Ohio Supreme Court. They stated that the federal court did not have the authority to arrest and try them because the Fugitive Slave Law of 1850 was unconstitutional. But the Ohio Supreme Court upheld the constitutionality of the law by a three-to-two ruling. Because a black person had no rights. Black people were only three-fifths human.

_____

* The official record of the speech states: [Great and prolonged applause, in spite of the efforts of the Court and the Marshal to silence it.] Extract from Charles Langston's Speech at the Cuyahoga County Courthouse, Cleveland, Ohio, May 12, 1859. From the records of Oberlin College, Oberlin, Ohio.

So although the Chief Justice of the Ohio Supreme Court personally opposed slavery, he wrote that his judicial duty left him no choice but to acknowledge that an Act of the United States Congress was the supreme law of the land and he had to uphold it. Outraged, the abolitionist community held a huge rally at which John Mercer, the sole black speaker, made a fiery address in support of the cause and of his brother. As a result, political leaders in Ohio were voted out and, in 1859, 'rescue' allies who attended the Ohio Republican convention (the Republican Party was anti-slavery, the Democrats were pro-slavery) succeeded in making the repeal of the Fugitive State Law of 1850 part of the party platform. This was the convention that would nominate Abraham Lincoln for President.

The Ohio-Wellington rescue radicalised many people, including one young black man, Lewis Sheridan Leary. But Sheridan Leary had had enough of rescues, and courts, and laws, and political conventions. He decided to go further. Leary was part of a long line of black men and women in the United States, Canada, Latin and South American, the Caribbean and Africa who revolted against slavery.

Some of the most well-known slave revolts are: 1712 New York Slave Revolt, New York City; 1733 St. John Slave Revolt, Saint John; 1739 Stono Rebellion, South Carolina; 1741 New York Conspiracy, New York City;

1760 Tacky's War, Jamaica; 1800 Gabriel Prosser, Virginia; 1805 Chatham Manor, Virginia; 1811 German Coast Uprising, Territory of Orleans; 1815 George Boxley, Virginia; 1822 Denmark Vesey, South Carolina; 1831 Nat Turner's Rebellion, Virginia; 1831–1832 Baptist War, Jamaica, all suppressed.

And the one victory: 1791–1804, the Haitian Revolution-Saint-Domingue.

Years before Waterloo, Toussaint L'Ouverture and his nation had defeated Napoleon at a time when the Emperor of the French was thought to be unconquerable.

The story of Haiti would have been known to Lewis Sheridan Leary. This may have been one of the reasons he decided to join a man by the name of John Brown, a charismatic white preacher who dedicated his life to freeing slaves and ending slavery by any means necessary. He and his sons rode all over the territory of Kansas, as well as Nebraska and Missouri. He was the epitome of the term 'bushwacker' – riding out of the woods from nowhere with guns blazing, freeing entire communities of black people and killing whoever stood in the way of what he considered to be a mission from God.

He was a legend among black people, and white people, too, especially those who hated him. They were determined to hang him, his sons, and his followers from the highest tree. But John Brown believed that killing in the name of freeing the enslaved was simply the Lord's work. He killed and burned and wreaked mayhem.

Finally, John Brown decided to settle the question of slavery once and for all. He would raid the federal arsenal at Harpers Ferry, West Virginia. After that, his plan was simple. He considered the Southern plantation owners effeminate, weak, and the Devil's people. His side was Righteous, in his own eyes, so the whole thing would be a walkover. He would raid the arsenal, use the rifles captured there, arm those of the enslaved who wanted to side with him, and then strike total fear into the slaveholders of Virginia.

On the first night he calculated that he could count on two to five hundred black rebels to rise up. He would make this happen by sending his agents to nearby plantations to rally support. Brown only planned to hold Harpers Ferry for a short time. With his followers, he would move rapidly southward, sending out armed bands along the way, freeing more people, foraging for food, stealing horses, taking hostages, all to destroy the morale of slaveholders. He would follow the ridge of the Appalachian Mountains into the heart of the South. That was the plan. John Brown had no doubt that he could make this succeed.

But this is what happened.

On Sunday night, 16 October 1859, he led his men

into the town of Harpers Ferry. The idea was to take hostage the great-grand nephew of George Washington and to capture some items of Washington's for their symbolic value. This was successful, as was the cutting of telegraph wires, slowing down an incoming train. Unfortunately and ironically, Brown's men shot a man who worked on the train – a black man. And the enslaved did not rebel while the townspeople began to fight back. Brown managed to capture the arsenal, taking his hostages inside of the armoury but he was soon surrounded. One of his sons went out to make a truce and was shot and killed; one of Brown's lieutenants panicked, tried to swim across the Potomac River and was shot dead by the townspeople who used his body for target practice.

Then Brown lost another son, and later that day, the President ordered the Marines under Robert E. Lee to take the armoury back. At Harpers Ferry, Lee tried to effect a surrender, but Brown refused. Lee's men broke in, and, helped by George Washington's great-grand nephew, they found John Brown. Lee wrote in his report after capturing Brown: 'The blacks, whom he [John Brown] forced from their homes in this neighbourhood, as far as I could learn, gave him no voluntary assistance.'

Lee, one of the geniuses of American military history, would resign his command a few years later in order to lead the Confederate forces during the Civil

War. John Brown was found guilty of treason against the Commonwealth of Virginia and was hanged, an act witnessed and praised by John Wilkes Booth, the actor and white supremacist who would later go on to assassinate President Lincoln. On the day of his execution, Brown wrote his last prophecy: 'I John Brown am now quite certain that the crimes of this guilty, [sic] land: [sic] will never be purged away; but with Blood.'

Even though the Oberlin community had been sceptical about the raid the trial had transformed Brown into a superstar and eventually a martyr. Though 'Harpers Ferry was insane', wrote the religious weekly the *Independent*, 'the controlling motive of his demonstration was sublime.'

Lewis Sheridan Leary, one of Brown's raiders, was mortally wounded while attempting to cross the Shenandoah River. His name is written on the Cenotaph Memorial at Oberlin, Ohio. He was twenty-four years old and had left behind his young, proud widow, Mary. Mary Patterson Leary Langston would tell her grandson, Langston, about John Brown, about the fight for freedom that he and her first husband had waged and how Langston's grandfather had played a part in it, too.

Freedom had been Langston's birthright.

CHAPTER TWO

'A NEW SONG', one of Langston's protest poems, was cited by Joseph McCarthy's Senate Committee as an example of Langston's 'Red' (communist) proclivities. But McCarthy would have been incapable of understanding this cry from Langston's heart, his need to lay out the landscape – real and poetic – of an ongoing atrocity.

The only way that he could fight it was to write it.

That the poem and other poems like it became a rope to lynch him was both evil and ironic:

'A New Song'
Bitter was the day, I say,
When the lyncher's rope
Hung about my neck,
And the fire scorched my feet,
And the oppressors had no pity,

Lynching – which involved kidnapping and often

burning the victim while still alive (other atrocities involved hanging, rape, pre- and post-mortem mutilation, and other acts of sexual violence) – was the main tool of racial terrorists like the white supremacist organisation the Ku Klux Klan. The hanging of black people as well as Native Americans and Jews was America's main human rights violation on its own soil from the 1880s until the end of the 1950s. Racist lynching was a direct result of the outcome of the conflagration known as the American Civil War, 1861–1865.

Lynching was used as one of the South's fight-backs after their defeat in the war. Southerners asserted their 'manhood' by terrorising black people who were trapped on the old plantations by local laws and their lack of mobility

By 1860 there were 3.5 million enslaved black people and 500,000 black people not enslaved ('free blacks') in the continental United States. During the presidential campaign of 1860, Abraham Lincoln had campaigned against the expansion of slavery beyond those states in which it already existed, but not against slavery itself. After he was elected President, seven states declared their secession from the Union before Lincoln even took office on 4 March 1861. The incoming administration rejected the legality of secession, considering it rebellion. Several other slave states then rejected calls for secession at this point. The

South Carolina planter John Townsend, speaking shortly after Lincoln's election, stated: 'Our enemies are about to take possession of the government, that they intend to rule us according to the caprices of their fanatical theories ...'

One Alabama secessionist stated that, if black and white people lived together as equals in the South, 'We ourselves (white people) would become the executioners of our own slaves. To this extent would the policy of our Northern enemies drive us; and thus would we not only be reduced to poverty, but what is still worse, we should be driven to crime, to the commission of sin.'

The North and South saw one another as living in different realities, different worlds. This feeling had increased between 1800 and 1860. By the end of the 1850s the North was a manufacturing powerhouse, fast-moving, a place where immigrants and free black people lived in relative freedom, where a single woman could live on her own without being stigmatised, a place where a person could change their identity and become new. The decision in the Dred Scott case was seen as a perversion of the Constitution by the North. On the other hand, the South imagined itself to be like an England that never was: genteel, romantic, a place of chivalry that relied on agrarian slave labour and subsistence farming done by poor whites, 'the lower class'.

Abolitionists called the South 'the slave power'.

Lincoln had warned about this power in his famous 'A House Divided' speech in 1858: a house divided against itself cannot stand. His speech struck a chord in the North. Many Northerners saw slavery not as a moral or a human rights issue, but as a Southern threat to the idea of American republicanism itself. Slaveholding states tended towards autonomy. They were like kingdoms, fiefdoms. Northeners believed that only the labour of a free people could ensure the existence of the United States of America. The South's dependence and addiction to slavery included with it an autonomy which disconnected it from any real idea and desire for the Union. This set it on a doomed collision course with the North.

Great Britain backed the South largely for economic reasons. Southern cotton was one of its economic drivers. If the South left the Union, going its own way, theoretically parts of the United States could be re-occupied by the old colonial masters. This would not be tolerated. The union of the states – the United States – had to survive.

It is important to remember that Abraham Lincoln's primary goal was to save the Union: the United States of America. If he could have done this without freeing black people he would have done so. At 4:30 a.m. on 12 April 1861, those Southern states, which had seceded from the Union and called themselves the Confederate States of America, opened fire on the United States military installation at Fort Sumter, South Carolina. Lincoln responded by calling for a volunteer army from each state to recapture federal property. This led to declarations of secession by four more slave states. Lincoln had taken office on 4 March 1861. Both sides raised armies as the Union assumed control of the border states early in the war and a naval blockade was established.

In 1863, in an effort to break the South, Lincoln issued the Emancipation Proclamation which freed the enslaved in areas held by the Confederacy. At the same time, he managed to persuade Great Britain officially to stay out of the war. But slavery in the South helped to keep the Industrial Revolution in Britain going. The Southern cotton industry, 'King Cotton', was so important to it that individuals secretly continued to channel funds to the rebel South while the British government looked the other way. After the victory of the North, Britain was forced to pay the US millions in indemnity. In backing the South to win, Britain had made the wrong bet. The question of slavery, black emancipation, and black revolution was one that it faced, too.

On 1 August 1834, slavery was ended in Jamaica by the passing of the Slavery Abolition Act 1833, which led to emancipation on 1 August 1838. This was the date, on paper, that former slaves could choose their work and who they worked for. They gained the right to vote, too, but the poll tax was so high that they were effectively disenfranchised. A petition of complaint was sent to Queen Victoria in 1865. She replied that the Jamaican people should work harder and pray. Jamaican women took to the market place to demand freedom for their people.

Two Jamaican patriots decided to take matters into their own hands. George William Gordon began to encourage the people to find ways to express their grievances. A church deacon, Paul Bogle, took his advice. On 7 October 1865, a black man was put on trial and convicted of trespassing on a long-abandoned plantation. This was the last straw for the people. An altercation broke out, and as a result, Paul Bogle discovered that there was a warrant out for his arrest. After marching to protest at Morant Bay, a volunteer militia opened fire, causing the black protestors to fight back, killing several white people. Governor Eyre, who ran the colony in the name of the Crown, hunted down the patriots, including Paul Bogle and brought them back to Morant Bay. In the aftermath, hundreds of black men and women were killed indiscriminately and executed, and over 600 people were flogged, including pregnant women.

The Jamaican patriot, Mrs Letitia Geoghagan, who was the first to rouse the people, was hung along with five other women. Victorian England was divided between those who thought it was horrendous that women, subjects of the Crown, had been hung; and those who thought it was horrendous that women, subjects of the Crown, had got involved at all.

Paul Bogle, his brother William, and George William Gordon, whose social eminence and respect were his sole crimes – Eyre felt threatened by him – were all hung. Today, Paul Bogle and George William Gordon have been given the designation 'National Hero Of Jamaica'.

The great and the good in Britain were torn into rival factions over Jamaica's 'Morant Bay Rebellion' and its aftermath and whether the governor of Jamaica should be put on trial for murder. Charles Dickens was opposed to a trial for murder. Charles Darwin supported it.

The governor never went to trial.

While the UK faced revolt at Morant Bay, America, between 1865 and 1870, added three amendments to the American Constitution, amendments which changed the lives of African Americans forever. These were the Thirteenth, Fourteenth and Fifteenth Amendments.

The Thirteenth Amendment immediately abolished and continues to prohibit slavery. It was passed in 1864 and adopted at the end of 1865, after the assassination of Abraham Lincoln earlier that year. It states in part: 'Neither slavery nor involuntary servitude, except as a punishment for crime whereof the party shall have been duly convicted, shall exist within the United States, or any place subject to their jurisdiction.' (Langston Hughes was born thirty-seven years to the day after Abraham Lincoln, through Congress, ended slavery in the United States). Each state was required to ratify the amendment. After rejecting it in 1865, the state of Mississippi, where my late father, Ben, was born, grew up and a great deal of my family still live, did not ratify the Thirteenth Amendment outlawing slavery until ... 16 March 1995.

The Fourteenth Amendment came into being on 9 July 1868. It states in part: 'All persons born or naturalized in the United States, and subject to the jurisdiction thereof, are citizens of the United States and of the State wherein they reside. No State shall make or enforce any law which shall abridge the privileges or immunities of citizens of the United States; nor shall any State deprive any person of life, liberty, or property, without due process of law; nor deny to any person within its jurisdiction the equal protection of the laws.'

The Fifteenth Amendment was ratified in 1870. It states: 'The right of citizens of the United States to vote shall not be denied or abridged by the United States or by any State on account of race, colour, or previous condition of servitude.'

These amendments are called the 'Reconstruction

Amendments' and were meant not only to address the situation of black people born on the soil of the United States, but to begin the process of healing after the war, which had left the South demoralised and devastated. These amendments have never been taken out of the Constitution, but only after President Lyndon Baines Johnson signed the series of bills which make up the Civil Rights Act of 1964 – the result of the struggle of millions to attain justice – did these amendments fully serve all of the citizens of the United States.

But in spite of the Civil War and the new amendments to the Constitution, by the time that Charles Henry Langston had settled in Kansas, everything was being reversed. The bright future that black people and their supporters had seen right after the war had begun to fade. This is one of the tragedies of American history. It was in the 1870s that the rollback started. A combination of political and economic forces allowed conservatives and racists to reverse hard-won gains. These forces destroyed the momentum that the Civil War and Reconstruction had created. In the Southern states, black people were forced back into a state of slavery in all but name. They became sharecroppers – tenant farmers – in conditions that made it impossible for them to progress, even to leave the land without fear and the threat and reality of death. The old blues song 'All God's Chillen Got Shoes' is about the desire to just be able to walk, go where you want, be free. At this time, the Ku Klux Klan came into being as a white supremacist, conservative Christian terrorist organisation created to enforce the state laws and customs of segregation, all of which violated the US Constitution, allowing 'Jim Crow' to reign.

Jim Crow refers to the laws, practices and customs designed to render black people not quite human, put them back at the bottom of the heap and keep them there. The name Jim Crow comes from a white minstrel character whose face is painted the colour of a crow – black, thereby stereotyping and ridiculing black people. Until 1964, it was possible to find the policy of Jim Crow somewhere in the US. It lasted for almost 100 years. The price of Jim Crow to people of African descent, to the US itself through the loss and destruction of human initiative, brainpower and drive cannot be calculated. From the decade after the end of the Civil War, all of the rights that Charles Henry Langston had dedicated his life to practically disappeared.

Racism had become institutionalised often to an insane degree. The state of Louisiana was particularly involved in what is called 'sangularity', the 'measuring' of African blood in an individual. The categories of sangularity were: mulatto – one black parent, one white parent; quadroon – one white grandparent, one African grandparent; octoroon – one white great-grandparent, one African great-grandparent. A bit like grading a dog or cat. Each of these degrees of sangularity had its own societies and was treated differently. Quadroons often looked white and there was a famous 'Quadroon Ball' in New Orleans where men could go and ogle the blonde, blue-eyed, ivory-skinned girls who were not 'quite white'. Needless to say, black men were not allowed to these parties!

The South – and the North in time – began to set up a system known as 'separate but equal'. Under this system, black people technically had the same facilities, but they were separate and always inferior to those of whites. A citizen of New Orleans, Homer Plessy, decided to join a campaign challenging 'separate but equal'. He boarded a car of the East Louisiana Railroad and sat in the white section. This seemed normal to all around him until he announced – as planned – that he was an octoroon and had a black great-grandfather. He was promptly thrown off the train. He and his fellow campaigners set out to challenge 'separate but equal' as unconstitutional before the US Supreme Court, the highest court in the land. His court case: 'Plessy vs Ferguson' became a landmark. A terrible landmark.

In 1896 the Supreme Court ruled that 'separate but equal' was not unconstitutional. It stated that the Thirteenth, Fourteenth and Fifteenth Amendments only applied to governments, not to individuals.

The train company was owned by an individual. Therefore the amendments did not apply. This ruling immediately invalidated the Civil Rights Act of 1875 as well. The Chief Justice of the Supreme Court added: 'We consider the underlying fallacy of the plaintiff's argument to consist in the assumption that the enforced separation of the two races stamps the colored race with a badge of inferiority. If this be so, it is not by reason of anything found in the act, but solely because the colored race chooses to put that construction upon it.' In other words, if Homer Plessy saw racial segregation as something that degraded him as a human being and denied him his rights as an American citizen, that was simply his point of view. He had no remedy in law.

That was it. The Supreme Court was the end of the line.

Homer Plessy had no choice but to plead guilty to breaking the law and pay a fine. And generations of black people, millions of individuals were rendered non-citizens, less than human. The Supreme Court, in effect, had said so.

The black community's advancement ceased as far as the wider public arena was concerned. Booker T. Washington decided to make the best of a horrible situation. Washington, born in slavery to an enslaved African American mother and an unknown white father, became Principal of the all-black Tuskegee

Normal and Industrial Institute in Alabama, a college dedicated to teaching black people to become skilled workers. Washington decided that self-help was the way forward and issued the 'Atlanta Compromise' which accepted black isolation from white society. A brilliant and able workaholic on behalf of his people, he was also a man who did not rock the boat, making him one of the most celebrated individuals of the age. But he and his students, all black people, now lived in a country in which all of the legislation passed to set them free and put them on the road to recovery after the Civil War had been effectively set aside. The Supreme Court underlined this by limiting the federal government's right to intervene in state law. States which had successfully integrated elements of their society abruptly adopted oppressive legislation, erasing Reconstruction, making it seem as if it had never happened.

And Jim Crow spread North as black people began to leave the oppression of the South. All over the country, separate but equal became the law. But separate was never equal. African Americans filed lawsuit after lawsuit, but every one of them failed. White militias were set up to enforce Jim Crow. Scientific theories came into vogue comparing African people to apes. To speak against any of this was to risk assault, or much worse. It is the truth, even today, that to be born with black skin can limit your educational opportunities, damage your mental and physical health, and shorten your life.

Two days after the birth of Langston Hughes, Charles Lindberg, the first man to fly solo across the Atlantic, was born. At the end of the same month that Langston and Charles Lindberg were born, John Steinbeck, like Langston destined to become a great American writer, was born, too. It is safe to say that the fate of these three baby boys, born so closely together, was largely determined by the colour of their skin.

Langston Hughes, a naturally free spirit, was handed a life already shaped by society before he had the chance to shape it himself. This is what Langston knew from an early age.

The story of the Langston Family – of all African American families – has been infected by the tragedy of the 1870s to 1900. The wounds are ancient, toxic and buried deep inside the psyche of the African American. A dysfunctional template had been created and reinforced by a century-long combination of law, violence and the fear created by it. Some things cannot be excused. But many things can be explained by Plessy vs Ferguson.

Langston Hughes' work is an exploration of the courage found in the scarred landscape of the black soul.

He knew it intimately.

He was a Langston.

CHAPTER THREE

FROM *THE SELECTED POEMS* of *Langston Hughes*:
'Madam and the Rent Man'

> *The rent man knocked.*
> *He said, Howdy-do?*
> *I said, What*
> *Can I do for you?*
> *He said, You know*
> *Your rent is due.*

There are no cosy, sitting-by-the-fireside tales about the family of Langston Hughes. Langston wrote about his grandmother in his autobiography *The Big Sea*, but it is largely accepted now that he embellished her portrait in his attempt to show black family life as warm and solid in itself. He was trying to build a case for the efficacy of black life in general on its own terms, in its own language. But first he had to find a way to bridge the gap between that life and the preconceptions that a white readership might bring. And so he 'created' his grandmother as a warm, wise person instead of the stern, highly educated woman that she really was, a woman wise and cynical in the ways of the nation that called itself 'the home of the free'.

She knew, and Langston was brought up to know, that the achievements of the Langston family against great odds would have made them extraordinary in any country at any moment in time. It was this self-knowledge that caused the Langstons to feel confident enough to become part of their time, and to contribute to the events of their time. Langston's own interest and knowledge of politics, his deep curiosity about other people and faraway lands, stemmed from the Langston tradition of engagement, of being in the world. His grandmother, in telling Langston how his family had come to make their home, not in the South where they had begun, but in the western states of Kansas and Missouri, would have told him this story:

A few days before Harpers Ferry, Charles Henry Langston met with John Brown. Brown told him that Kansas would be a good place for black people to settle. On 2 December 1859, John Brown was executed for treason. Black people and white abolitionists mourned throughout the country. On the day of his execution, ceremonies were held, particularly in Ohio where Charles Henry lived at the time. In Cleveland, Ohio, a huge ceremony took place in a hall draped in black highlighted with a large, gilt-edged portrait of John Brown. At the hour of his death, 2,000 mourners met to honour the great liberator. Charles Henry was there, too. The only black speaker at the event. He had made up his mind to take Brown's advice.

In April 1862, a year after the Civil War began, Charles Henry headed for Kansas. The same year that he arrived, Charles Henry organised a school for the children of 'contrabands' who had fled to the Union lines from the neighbouring state of Missouri. The word contraband, a French word that has been in the English language since the late sixteenth century, denotes any item which, during wartime, is considered illegal to possess or sell. Those former slaves who had fled to Union lines were declared 'contraband of war'. They were considered to be contraband because escaped enslaved people were legally the 'property' of their 'owners'. This policy of contraband of war, first articulated by General Benjamin Butler in 1861 in what came to be known as the Fort Monroe Doctrine, was applied to them, making it illegal for anyone other than their masters to 'possess' them before the Emancipation Proclamation.

With his school, Charles Henry took a great risk. In 1862, a year before the Proclamation, Charles Henry was teaching people who were considered 'stolen property'. But he accepted that risk and went on to teach in the school for about three years. The local paper of the time said: '… the school was gotten up by the efforts of C.H. Langston of Ohio who deserves great credit for his efforts. We hope that in the future his earnest labors will receive something like an adequate compensation.'

In 1863, Langston returned to Ohio to form with his younger brother John Mercer, the United States Colored Troops. Then from 1864 until 1870, Charles Henry worked for black suffrage in Kansas.

On 14 January 1864, he was sent to the Republican Party state convention, a great honour.

In 1865, Abraham Lincoln signed the Emancipation Proclamation, freeing the enslaved in all territories held by the Confederacy, with Union soldiers enforcing the Proclamation.

By the end of 1865, Charles Henry was given the job of running the Freedmen's Bureau. Its full name was The Bureau of Freedmen, Refugees and Abandoned Land. It was set up to prevent the South returning to slavery, and to enable the newly liberated to find work and receive an education. The Bureau also provided assistance for all of the poor in the newly liberated areas of the Confederacy. It was created an Act of Congress by the War Department in early 1865. Charles Henry's job was to aid the huge influx of black people into Kansas and Missouri. Langston's grandfather did not stop working on behalf of his people.

In 1872 he became Principal of the Quindaro Freedmen's School (later Western University), the first black college west of the Mississippi River. In 1880 he became president of a statewide 'Convention of Colored Men' that called on the Refugee Relief Board to donate 'monies and goods' for the new migrants and settle them on school properties to help them get established. He also served as associate editor of the *Historic Times*, a local paper that promoted the cause of equal rights and justice for blacks. Charles Henry Langston's accomplishments, combined with his own natural gifts, should have given him and his family a life of ease, a life of wealth, a life of safety. He thought that moving to the West might give him a chance to make a new and better life for himself and for his people. He moved there to escape racism. But he found it there nevertheless.

And so Langston Hughes, who is mainly associated with New York City and Harlem in particular, is also claimed as a son of Kansas, Nebraska and Missouri, and Ohio, too. These states today all honour Langston and his family. Langston knew the stories of these Western states and wrote about his life growing up as a black boy there. To be born and grow up there was much different from life in the South.

The area of the United States where Charles Henry Langston settled is known as the Great Plains, and is the area where Kansas and Missouri are located. It is a broad expanse of steppe, prairie and grassland lying west of the Mississippi River and east of the Rocky Mountains. The Plains stretch all the way to Canada, and were home to buffalo before white settlers hunted them to relative extinction. They contained, and still do, Native American nations, as well as their sacred places and hunting grounds. The Lakota, Northern Cheyenne and Arapaho nations, for example, have their sacred lands in the Black Hills of South Dakota. It was there, in the Black Hills, near the Little Big Horn River, that the combined might of these indigenous nations wiped out George Armstrong Custer and the 7th Calvary in a battle that lasted no more than half an hour but went on to attain legendary status as Custer's Last Stand.

In the Civil War and post-war era, the African American population grew rapidly in Kansas. They were concentrated in the towns and rural areas in the eastern part of the state, close to Missouri, in the towns of Leavenworth, Lawrence and Topeka. The largest group settled in Leavenworth, making it not surprising that Lincoln University, one of America's foremost black universities, was founded there. The school was created in 1866 by black soldiers in order to educate black children. In 1954, when American schools were being desegegrated, Lincoln opened its doors … to white students.

By 1880 Charles Henry was president of the Convention of Colored Men, but exhausted and dispirited by the back-stabbing of some members of the black community, he decided to bow out of active public life. He had purchased a farm near Lawrence, close to Lakeview and the Kansas River in 1868. The following year he had married Mary Patterson Leary, the widow of Lewis Sheridan Leary, who brought their little daughter Louise Leary to the marriage. Mary was thrilled to be marrying into the prestigious Langston family and saw a bright future ahead for herself and her little daughter with a man she not only loved and deeply admired, but who was also a living legend. Charles Henry and Mary had two children of their own: a son, Nathaniel Turner Langston, named after Nat Turner, the African American freedom fighter who had led his fellow slaves in a revolt in the early part of the century which had struck fear throughout the white South; and a daughter, Caroline Mercer Langston. Known as 'Carrie', she became the mother of Langston Hughes. Charles Henry and Mary also fostered a boy whom they named Dessalines Langston, after one of the major leaders of the Haitian Revolution. Charles Henry and Mary didn't just work for black liberation, they gave their sons the names of black heroes.

The black leaders of Kansas asked Charles Henry if he would allow his name to be put into nomination for Lieutenant Governor of the state of Kansas at the Republican convention in September 1880. They were incensed that no black person had been considered. Charles Henry consented, but did not win the nomination. He returned to his farm and bought a share in a grocery business. One of the great African American leaders of the nineteenth century finally settled down to being a shopkeeper. In time he sold his farm and his business and moved himself and his family to a house in Alabama Street in Lawrence, Kansas, the house and street that Langston would come to know so well and which was where his literary life began.

Charles Henry, who had been suffering 'chronic stomach trouble', as his death certificate stated, died at home on 21 November 1892, nine years before Langston's birth. It was only recently that the graves of Charles Henry Langston and Mary Langston were given headstones. Today this great man is remembered for all of his extraordinary achievements. He left his grandson Langston an enormous legacy of service.

Charles Henry never knew Langston. He also never knew that his daughter, Langston's mother Carrie, had such an artistic soul! Carrie loved poetry and wrote it, too. She also adored the theatre. She loved the open road and transferred her love of it to her son. Carrie loved books and was fascinated by the Interstate Library Association that her father, Charles Henry, had founded. She always considered it to be a kind of home for her. Both of her husbands – Langston's father and the man she married after their divorce – left her in dire straits. She was constantly moving around, looking for work. It was as if she set out to defy what a black woman could do at the time, knock down what a black woman was expected to be. In doing so Carrie was Charles Henry's child, like him, a rejecter of 'the way things were supposed to be'. She appeared on stage at Oberlin. She appeared, too, in and out of her son's life.

Carrie Mercer Langston Hughes existed as a kind of free spirit in treacherous times for African Americans. Life was brutal for her, but she also seemed to drift through life in a dream. Although being a black woman with no money, the dream was constantly, rudely interrupted. She was beautiful and absent and disconnected and Langston romanticised her because it was the only way that he could deal with her.

The way of the poet.

She would send him begging letters after he became famous and warned him that his father, living in Mexico and not in contact, might someday do the same. She was unaware that the man had become relatively wealthy. Langston sent his mother money

42

until the day she died in 1938. She never really took the kind of responsibility that convention dictated she should. Always poor, always on the edge, she did things the 'Carrie' way. Perhaps she contributed to the making of a great artist. Or perhaps she made Langston the loner that he essentially was.

At some point and somewhere, Carrie had met an arrogant man full of overweening pride by the name of James Nathaniel Hughes. Like her, James Nathaniel was full of dreams, both of them living in a land which would not allow them to have dreams. After James Nathaniel Hughes left her and little Langston in pursuit of the dreams denied him, Carrie moved to the town of Joplin, Missouri. She was still a Langston, still capable of living free in the matrix of the black community. Sometimes Langston stayed with her, sometimes he did not. He grew used to this in real life. But in his poetic life – where he really lived – there existed a wise, stable, maternal woman, always there, always present. His mother.

Caroline Mercer Langston Hughes would journey through her own universe, back and forth, round and round all of her life. She defined herself in her own terms. After all, this was what her uncle James Mercer Langston and her father Charles Henry Langston and her mother Mary Leary Langston, living with the ghost of her young first husband Sheridan Leary, had set out to do.

To be true to oneself was the message of her son's work.

The poetry of Langston Hughes was written by a poet who had come from a free people.

CHAPTER FOUR

THE FIRST CHILD BORN to Carrie and James Nathaniel Hughes died when he was a few months old. This was not unusual in those days for black, urban mothers. Poor nutrition, a substandard existence in dirty, disease-ridden and overcrowded cities, the very stress of racism were some of the factors that contributed to African American infant mortality.

Langston himself was a small man. He was born on 1 February 1902, in Joplin, Missouri, a city on the Mississippi River. James Mercer Langston Hughes was given the first name of 'James' after his father, and 'Mercer Langston' as middle names, after his famous great-uncle and his mother. Later, Langston was to drop his first two names and simply call himself Langston Hughes.

At the time of his birth Langston's father was studying to be a lawyer. Black people, however, were forbidden to practise law in the state of Missouri, as well as most of the states of the Union, so James

Nathaniel Hughes set out to challenge this in court. On the day that Langston was born.

James Nathaniel Hughes began as he meant to continue, setting a pattern of absence that lasted for the rest of his son's life.

Carrie, who was teaching in a school and wrote poetry from time to time, was delighted with her new son. He looked strong and robust, and he looked like a Langston. Carrie was content with her work and life, but James Nathaniel Hughes wanted more. Even though he was light-skinned and therefore considered to be of higher status than dark-skinned black people, both he – and Carrie, too – had to suffer the discrimination which kept them from better positions. James Nathaniel had taken correspondence courses in law but was denied a chance to take the bar exam, first in Oklahoma, then in Missouri. Eventually, unable to live under the restrictions an African American was subjected to, James Nathaniel made up his mind to seek his fortune and just desserts elsewhere. He packed up and left Carrie and Langston in dire poverty when Langston was a small boy. Except for a handful of times, Langston never saw him or had contact with him again.

There was a time when Langston and Carrie travelled to Mexico to see James Nathaniel, doing very well south of the border. His mother and father tried to reconcile but Carrie couldn't take Mexico and James Nathaniel's arrogant attitude, so she and Langston returned to the Great Plains. When they got back to Missouri, Carrie realised that she could no longer afford to live in Joplin and began to move around looking for work. In his autobiography *The Big Sea* Langston describes those early years with his mother:

When I first started to school, I was with my mother a while in Topeka. (And later, for a summer in Colorado, and another in Kansas City.) She was a stenographer for a colored lawyer in Topeka, named Mr. Guy. She rented a room near his office, downtown. So I went to a 'white' school in the downtown district.

At first, they did not want to admit me to the school, because there were no other colored families living in that neighborhood. They wanted to send me to the colored school, blocks away down across the railroad tracks. But my mother, who was always ready to do battle for the rights of a free people, went directly to the school board, and finally got me into the Harrison Street School – where all the teachers were nice to me, except one who sometimes used to make remarks about my being colored. And after such remarks, occasionally the kids would grab stones and tin cans out of the alley and chase me home.

But there was one little white boy who would always take up for me. Sometimes others of my classmates would, as well. So I learned early not to hate all white people. And ever since, it has seemed to me that most people are generally good, in every race and in every country where I have been.*

When she could, Carrie took her son to see plays, and to acquaint him with the world of books:

My mother used to take me to see all the plays that came to Topeka like *Buster Brown*, *Under Two Flags*, and *Uncle Tom's Cabin*. We were very fond of plays and books. Once we heard *Faust* …

… In Topeka, as a small child, my mother took me with her to the little vine-covered library on the grounds of the Capitol. There I first fell in love with librarians, and I have been in love with them ever since – those very nice women who help you find wonderful books! The silence inside the library, the big chairs, and long tables, and the fact that the library was always there and didn't seem to have a mortgage on it, or any sort of insecurity about it – all of that made me love it. And right then, even before I was six, books began to happen to me, so that after

* An edited extract from From *The Big Sea* © The Estate of Langston Hughes.

a while, there came a time when I believed in books more than in people – which, of course, was wrong. That was why, when I went to Africa, I threw all the books into the sea.*

While at primary school, Langston was elected the class poet. He wrote later that at first he thought that he was given the honour because of his race, since poets should have rhythm. Soon he was writing poetry, short stories, plays. He wrote for the school newspaper. He wrote everything he could.

But Langston Hughes was primarily a poet and this was what he considered himself to be.

Carrie often had to leave Langston behind as she went out in search of work. He was raised largely by his grandmother. Later in life, Langston would cite his grandmother Mary as a major influence on his work and his life. He glorified her as a warm, loving woman who never cried. The truth was that she was as hard as nails and did not suffer fools. She had continued her tradition of marrying men who fought for African American civil rights by marrying Charles Henry Langston. But although she had married a prominent man in black political circles and she herself had a college degree – the first African American woman to attain one – Mary was still female, black,

---

* From *The Big Sea* © The Estate of Langston Hughes.

49

and therefore barred from earning a decent salary.

But to Langston, she was a living legend.

She was an example of the brilliance and resiliency that he saw in all black people, the epitome of what Langston's friend, Ernest Hemingway, called 'grace under pressure'. Grace under pressure was how black people survived, as far as Langston was concerned. His own father could not attain and demonstrate this grace but his grandmother could and did. She became his inspiration:

'My grandmother raised me until I was twelve,' he wrote later in his life. 'Sometimes I saw my mother, but not often. … You see, my grandmother was very proud, and she would never beg or borrow from anybody … My grandmother looked like an Indian – with very long black hair. She said she could lay claim to Indian land, but that she never wanted the government (or anybody else) to give her anything. She said there had been a French trader who came down the St Lawrence, then on foot to the Carolinas, and mated with her grandmother, who was a Cherokee – so all her people were free. … She sat, looking very much like an Indian, copper-colored with long black hair, just a little grey in places at seventy, sat in her rocker and read the Bible, or held me on her lap and told me long, beautiful stories about people who wanted to make the Negroes free, and how her father had had apprenticed to him many slaves in Fayetteville, North Carolina, before the war, so that they could work out their freedom under him as stone masons. And once they had worked out their purchase, he would see that they reached the North, where there was no slavery.

"Through my grandmother's stories always life moved, moved heroically toward an end. Nobody ever cried in my grandmother's stories. They worked, or schemed, or fought. But no crying. When my grandmother died, I didn't cry, either. Something about my grandmother's stories (without her ever having said so) taught me the uselessness of crying about anything."*

He dedicated an early poem 'Aunt Sue's Stories' to her and his beloved Auntie Mary Read, who took him in when his grandmother died and his mother was away working. Carrie's experience was one of the reasons that Langston dedicated himself to the working class, their concerns, their struggles, their injustices … and also to their joy. It is his grandmother who is the inspiration for 'Aunt Hagar', an elderly washerwoman who treated her neighbours with holistic medicines that invariably cured them, in his first novel *Not Without Laughter*.

---

* Edited extract from *The Big Sea* © The Estate of Langston Hughes

Through his grandmother Langston demonstrated that ordinary black people, their way of speaking and living, had great value in and of itself. It was his grandmother who gave him a love of the oral tradition of black culture. Storytelling and the art of it are at the heart of Langston Hughes's work, work that cries out to be spoken, to be read aloud. While his mother worked in restaurants, steel mills, hotels, anywhere she could find work, and his father, James Nathaniel, had vanished, Langston was left in the care of an old woman who transmitted her knowledge and wisdom through the spoken word.

His grandmother refused to take in washing or cook like other black women did to make ends meet. A proud woman, instead, she would rent rooms to university students, sometimes moving out of her own house in order to rent to groups of them. She always lived in fear of foreclosure which meant that Langston sometimes had little to eat. His grandmother Mary was always saving to pay the mortgage.

In his poem 'Mother to Son', one of the most famous poems in the African American canon, a woman says: 'Well, son, I tell you/Life for me ain't been no crystal stair.'

Langston began to write poetry after his grandmother's death in about 1915 when he was thirteen years old. He recalled in his autobiography the small 'monkey-stove' that his mother kept in the rented room that they lived in together after Grandmother Mary died. The stove was used for both heating and cooking. His mother would send him through the alleys to find discarded boxes to bring home to burn for kindling. They would often have to use a hatchet to break the boxes after she had returned at night from work, making a great deal of noise. Carrie warned him to be careful of what she called 'long-branch kindling', a piece of board placed on top of the stove. If the kindling broke off and fell on the rug, it could start a fire.

And there were times that he could not live with his mother because she was moving around and he had to somehow live on his own. They moved together to Cleveland, Ohio, to a house that eventually had to be sold in foreclosure at a sheriff's auction in 1918.

Recently, a group of community activists in Cleveland set out to save one of the houses in which Langston had rented a room as a teenager. It was located in what was, in Langston's time, an upmarket black neighbourhood. He would often speak about how a room in a house in Cleveland had inspired him to become a writer. During the recent housing crisis in the United States, the house had been designated for demolition. A librarian at the Cleveland Public Library heard about it, and set out to save the property. The community activists became involved when one of them learned that Langston had decided to stay behind there after his mother moved on. Langston took on the rent for the small room he had shared with his mother, managed to stay in school and work after in a local department store. Langston wrote about living in a small room in Cleveland, eating rice and hot dogs every night, and reading, reading, reading. He eventually lived in a few different places in Cleveland. But thanks to the efforts of the activists and the Cleveland Public Library along with others, one of Langston's many addresses will become a home again, complete with a memorial garden next door.

While Langston was living in Cleveland, Carrie had married for a second time to a man by the name of Homer Clark by whom she had another son, Langston's stepbrother. Carrie would speak to Langston about his father, James Nathaniel, but would seldom tell him anything flattering. And since his father was not in his life, Langston knew very little about the Hughes side, only the little that his father told him during the brief times that they saw one another throughout James Nathaniel's life.

James Nathaniel Hughes lived in another world from Langston's and Carrie's. He lived in a sunny free world while Langston's world was full of cold Midwestern winters, and fear. There is no record that James Nathaniel Hughes ever really cared. Langston comforted himself by remembering his grandmother's stories and imagining that someday he would do something as important as her first husband Sheridan Leary had done. Maybe then his father would care.

But he never did.

There were those who said, later on in Langston's life, that he was always surrounded by people. And yet, even then, he seemed alone.

It was in Cleveland that Langston became utterly committed to books. Here he first became aware that the most dependable thing he had was his writing. He would always remain true – not necessarily to individual works or poems – but to writing, to poetry itself. In Cleveland, too, he faced the fact that someday he would go back to Mexico to confront the man he had been named after. When he did, what would he say? Would he accuse him of leaving him and his mother to make their own way in the world? Would he beg him to come back to them – to him? Or would he ask his father if he could stay with him, live his life, too?

The poet in Langston knew the answer to his questions. But he was not yet able to write the poems.

CHAPTER FIVE

THERE WERE MANY AFRICAN AMERICANS who did respond to racism with the resilience and humour that Langston celebrated. For many, racism created a sense of self-hatred that extended out to hatred for other black people. Powerlessness and impotence in the face of repeated humiliation and violence was more that many could bear.

James Nathaniel Hughes, Langston's father, acutely felt this sense of being at the power and mercy of others. He hated whites, but he also hated African Americans and Native Americans, too. He was like the person who blames the victim of an assault for the crime instead of the perpetrator.

The African American poet Gwendolyn Brooks, remembered Langston saying once that he believed that his father hated all black people. Langston believed that James Nathaniel hated himself for having been born 'a Negro'. Langston told her that his father hated black people, hated his own family because they were black, and by extension, must have hated himself, too. He had studied to be a lawyer, but racism prevented him from taking up his profession. He wanted his due. He wanted his respect. Instead of celebrating the birth of his second child, a baby who looked like he might live, James Nathaniel, a shopkeeper who had studied law and demanded that he be allowed to be a lawyer, was away asserting his rights, seeking his respect.

Langston's childhood and boyhood were father-less. It took immense courage, drive and focus to survive.

In Mexico James Nathaniel thought that his light-brown skin would enable him to blend in and therefore make the money and gain the respect and attention that he felt he deserved. He did indeed became a successful cattle rancher. But he gave his family nothing. James Nathaniel Hughes was a cold man, but this did not stop his son Langston dreaming about what his life must be like. When he was a little boy, Langston thought of his father as a big, strong cowboy in a Mexican sombrero. In this imaginary Mexico, a land of wonder and possibilities, James Nathaniel would be going back and forth from his business in the city to the vast ranch he owned in the mountains, and where he lived as a free man. There were no white people there to create racial barriers, and no landlords demanding the rent.

There are some Langston Hughes scholars who believe that the abandonment by his father had a profound effect on Langston's life and work. On some deep level, they conjecture, Langston was trying all of his life to prove to his father that black people were human beings and that their culture, their very essence, was worthy of respect, even emulation. Langston loved black people and often said that the fact that his father did not caused him a great deal of pain. His alleged contemplation of suicide might be one indication of this.

Perhaps the other indications are two works, both of which are called 'Mulatto'. One was a poem published in a collection in 1926, and the other a play produced in the early thirties. In the poem 'Mulatto' the father is a white slave owner, the rapist of a black woman. Out of crime was born their son, the 'Mulatto' of the title. Part of the voice of the poem, that of the son, gracefully morphs into the voice of the mother, the black woman standing between her rapist and their innocent son. Langston enters the consciousness of the white father/rapist and has him deep in reverie about the woods where he met the black woman, the closeness of nature there: 'The Southern night/Full of stars./Great big yellow stars.'

But Langston leaves the white father in his dreaming and returns to the mulatto son and his much harsher life. He has the son struggling to assert his identity in the face of the hostility of his white half-brothers. They refute him: 'Niggers ain't my brother' is the response the black boy receives from his white half-brothers. Langston then demonstrates the madness of racism. The black son looks more like his white father than his white half-brothers do. (The way that Langston's great-uncle, Gideon, so resembled his father that he took his last name.) To Langston, this juxtaposition of the dual reality of black and white in America, its erotic closeness, is the entire point of 'Mulatto'.

When confronted, the white father escapes into his memories again, leaving his mulatto son to scream: 'I am your son, white man!' But the father cannot hear. He is away with his own dreams, his own thoughts.

Today, the eminent Paris-based African-American poet, James Emmanuel, applauds Langston's ability – in this very early work – to enter the subconscious of other people, to go into the minds of others.

The second work that Langston entitled 'Mulatto' (full title: *Mulatto: A Play of the Deep South*, later renamed *The Barrier*) was written in the early thirties and produced on Broadway in 1935. The play is now considered old-fashioned and flawed. Nevertheless this melodrama may hold some autobiographical clues that point to Langston's relationship with James Nathaniel. The play revolves around Colonel Thomas Norwood, a white plantation owner; Cora, the black woman by whom he has several children, and Robert, the mulatto son of Thomas and Cora. Unlike Langston's white great-great-grandfather, Ralph Quarles, the fictional Norwood does not make a life with Cora and their children. Quite the opposite. Norwood does everything he can to reject the situation. But Robert is a young man who stands up for his rights, and the whites in the town see him as trouble. When he refuses to back down Norwood threatens him with a cane. He tells Robert to stop talking like a white man and talk like what he is. Robert tells him that what he is, is his son.

Enraged, Norwood pulls a gun. Robert disarms him and kills him.

Cora begs Robert to escape to the woods. By now driven mad by the tragedy of her life, Cora talks to Norwood's corpse, telling him that she knows that he is not really there in his dead body, but out with the other white people baying for Robert's blood – their son's blood. It is in Cora's monologue to Norwood's corpse, a powerful speech to give to a black woman in a Broadway theatre of the 1930s, that Langston lays out his case about the African American condition. Robert, before the whites can get to him and lynch him, kills himself with the one bullet left in his gun.

It is in parts of the dialogue in *Mulatto* that there might be some evidence of how Langston experienced his father and to some extent his mother. Cora, when explaining Robert's rebellious attitude says: 'He don't mean nothin' – just smart and young and eighteen.' Norwood telling Robert: 'Nigger women don't know the fathers. You're a bastard.' Cora to Norwood: 'Why don't you get up and stop 'em? He's your boy! … He's proud like you're proud.' And Norwood telling Cora that he doesn't want their children to be 'as dumb as the rest of these no-good darkies …'

This could be taken as proof of James Nathaniel's malevolent influence on Langston's work. But it is only a conjecture. It is important to remember that Langston was a poet – a great poet. The poetic imagination uses many elements in service of a poem, some may seem autobiographical when they are in fact not. Langston always used autobiography to paint the bigger picture. Without a doubt, James Nathaniel would have made up a great deal of Langston's emotional landscape, a father always does, whether present or absent, living or dead. But Langston never allowed his relationship with his father to turn him into his father: arrogant, angry, cold. He understood that part of what made up his father's hatred, his behaviour and attitude towards black people, towards the poor, was largely bred into him by the dire reality of black life in America.

Some overcame.

Some are overcome.

And some people, like James Nathaniel Hughes,

lived a self-denying existence that caused them to reject those they should love.

In the summer of 1919, for the first time in twelve years, Langston saw his father again. He was seventeen and had decided to seek him out. On the way there, while crossing the mighty Mississippi River, Langston wrote 'The Negro Speaks of Rivers':

> I've known rivers ancient as the world and older than the
> flow of human blood in human veins.
> My soul has grown deep like the rivers.
> I bathed in the Euphrates when dawns were young.
> I built my hut near the Congo and it lulled me to sleep.
> I looked upon the Nile and raised the pyramids above it.
> I heard the singing of the Mississippi when Abe Lincoln
> went down to New Orleans, and I've seen its muddy
> bosom turn all golden in the sunset
> I've known rivers:
> Ancient, dusky rivers.
> My soul has grown deep like the rivers.

But the glory and immortality that this poem would give Langston would have to wait. He had James Nathaniel Hughes to deal with.

In Mexico, Langston probably learned Spanish, a language he would eventually come to write in, as well as translate the works of others.

James Hughes thought that Langston's decision to

become a writer was a terrible one. He raged against the fact that the magazines that Langston submitted his work to did not pay, and that no one treated his son with the respect he deserved and expected – that a son of James Hughes should expect. He never let up on his contempt for black people: Langston later wrote that he couldn't understand why his father hated black people, because he loved black people very much.

In December of 1934, Langston returned to Mexico City. His father had died and Langston needed to take care of his business affairs. His father, who had done very well, and Langston, who would never make any serious money, had never reconciled their differences. When he got to Mexico City, Langston discovered that his father had disinherited him. But in a strange way, James Nathaniel Hughes had given him one gift: Mexico.

In addition to learning the language, Langston's mind had been filled with the colours and sounds of Mexico. Through his visits to his father, he could see that the whole world was available to him, not just America. After his father's death he began to write a children's story, a magical children's story called *The Pasteboard Bandit*, about two boys, one white, one Mexican. *The Pasteboard Bandit* was not discovered until 1992.

In many ways, it can be said that Langston had

no father. He certainly did not have one in the ways that matter to a child. Yet many people who went on to greatness, among them the 44th President of the United States, Barack Obama, did not know their fathers, or were rejected by them, or lived with them for a short time. Through the love and interest of their mothers, other family members, teachers and schools, community leaders, role models, through music, books, sport, art, religion and spirituality, many fatherless people – fatherless boys – have gone on to lead successful and useful lives, making valuable contributions to their families and to society.

Langston took the loss of his father and the suffering that it caused him, and extended it out to everyone who read or heard his work. He made his pain and loss a conduit through which he and his readers and listeners could expand their human capacity.

Did Langston ever forgive his father?

He may not have in life, but his work does, over and over again ...

Bitter was the day
When I bowed my back
Beneath the slaver's whip.
That day is past.

CHAPTER SIX

LANGSTON STAYED IN MEXICO in 1919 and taught English so that he could save money for university. He had a close call in Vera Cruz which almost became the last place he would ever see. A German brewmeister convinced himself that Langston and the woman the brewmeister fancied were having an affair. He called one day at the house Langston and the girl shared armed with a gun. The brewmeister shot the girl, Greta, four times, then went looking through the house for Langston. Langston happened to be out that afternoon. But if he had been there, the brewmeister could have ended the story of Langston Hughes right there in Vera Cruz.

Langston continued to submit essays and stories about Mexico to New York editors, determined to end up in Harlem, the city of his dreams. By the beginning of the 1920s, Harlem was the capital of African America – the seat of the most exciting and important cultural movement in the country: The Harlem

Renaissance. Langston longed to be there in spite of the fact that his father played his usual discouraging role in his life by telling him that a black man could not make it in America.

Langston set out to prove him wrong.

The June 1921 issue of the most important black journal in the nation, the *Crisis*, published his poem 'The Negro Speaks of Rivers'. Langston hoped that his idol, the brilliant black radical intellectual and writer, W.E.B. DuBois would notice it. DuBois was engaged quite simply in placing the African within world history, thereby re-calibrating history itself, especially Western European and American history. Langston desperately wanted his approval.

James Nathaniel agreed to finance Langston's studies at Columbia University in New York City for one year if Langston promised to study not literature but engineering. To his father, the idea of a black man living and working and thriving as a poet was completely insane. Langston happily agreed and sailed from Vera Cruz to the Big Apple.

Langston must have seen the illustrations of the typical 'Columbia man': smug, seated in a fine chair in his rooms, wearing a varsity sweater with a big 'C' emblazoned on it. There were some who said that the 'C' stood for something else, but Columbia men were nothing if not sure of their place in the world. And Langston was about to enter it.

The university was over 150 years old, ancient by American standards. Five Founding Fathers of the American nation had attended it. Columbia was also the school that awarded the most famous writing prize in the world outside of the Nobel: the Pulitzer Prize. Langston, like every American writer, wanted it.

Columbia is located in Morningside Heights, just below Harlem. That he would be so close to Harlem was part of the university's attraction for Langston. Although black students could attend Columbia, they were not allowed to live in the dormitories. When Langston turned up, the authorities tried to stop him moving in. But he had paid a deposit. Twelve other black students attended the university, however a Chinese student was the only student of colour in the dorms, and the only person who spoke to Langston. To complicate everything else, James Nathaniel's money had not arrived. The university gave Langston a few weeks to get it, or leave. He studied in a constant state of tension until the cash finally arrived with a lame excuse from James Nathaniel that something must have happened to it en route.

Langston quickly came to see that he did not have the proper clothes for the harsh New York winter. He had to ask his father to send him even more money. He dared not tell him that he was sending half of it to Carrie. In return, James Nathaniel demanded a strict accounting of Langston's expenditure, a cruel fore-shadowing of the way his writing patron would treat him a few years later.

In the end, Columbia turned out to be a horrible experience. The worry over his mother and the pressure from his father became too much. Langston decided to drop out of Columbia and sign on to a ship as a messman, basically a waiter and busboy.

Busboy and poet, Langston needed to see Africa:

I bathed in the Euphrates when dawns were young.
I built my hut near the Congo and it lulled me to sleep.
I looked upon the Nile and raised the pyramids above it.

Once in Africa, if he was lucky, he would see what he had imagined.

On 13 June 1923, Langston prepared for his voyage to Africa. He packed a large number of books to take with him to read when he wasn't serving food to the officers on board, but in the end he left his books behind. Books reminded him too much of Columbia, a place he wanted to forget. He was tired, too, of the daily grind of trying to have enough money to make ends meet, tired of the constant worry. Onboard ship, with the vast ocean before him, he could '… *fling my arms wide*', be free for the first time in his life.

The voyage took six months, calling at thirty-two different ports on the west coast of Africa. Langston journeyed up the Congo, a dream come true. He tried to connect with the Africans who worked on the ship for far less money than he did. But because of the light colour of his skin they called him a white man. He did his best to overcome that: he told them that he was their brother, that he wanted to observe their rituals, see how they really lived, create some kind of 'black solidarity'. They refused his overtures. They knew that he made thirty-five dollars a month while they made only six shillings for working much harder than he did. They also knew that his desire to be part of them did not extend to sharing their pay grade. Langston was heartily ashamed of himself for not speaking up on their behalf, but he needed every penny he made. He would always need money.

He signed on to another ship heading for Rotterdam. He loved every minute of his time there.

Back in New York Langston celebrated his twenty-second birthday with Countee Cullen, another writer he held in awe. Things were good. He was becoming known in literary circles. But he missed travelling so he signed on to another ship, but left it in Holland because of racist abuse. From there he took a train to Paris, the new 'Promised Land' for African Americans. The French, largely because of the presence in France of black soldiers in World War I, were in love with all things African, whether from the US, the Caribbean, South America – or Africa. He befriended four black British girls in town to study French. He wrote back home that he had fallen in love with one of them, Anne Marie Cousey. Anne Marie made up her mind that Langston was the man for her and asked him to come back to London with her and meet her family in Hampstead. Langston almost made the trip, but couldn't bring himself to do it. Instead he said goodbye and made his way to Venice where he ran out of money.

Alain Locke, a distinguished black writer and champion of his work, ran into him there and suggested that they return to Washington DC together. Langston could stay with him, Locke suggested, and he would use his influence to get him into Howard University, the most important black university in the land. Langston's great-uncle and namesake, James Mercer Langston, had been the first dean of Howard's law school. Langston thought it over. One thing that he knew for sure was that when he did return to university, it would be to a black one. As well as relieving his money worries if he lived with Locke, the man was also highly strategic within the literary circles Langston wanted to enter. Nevertheless, he told Locke that he would think it over.

Langston was pleasantly surprised when he returned to New York to discover that he had become a famous writer. Everyone who mattered wanted to know him, publish him. He thought that he might want to study psychology, sociology and history. He saw these studies as a way to make him a better writer, and help him better understand his people.

In the end, he did move to Washington DC, but not in with Locke. He wanted to make it on his own. Besides, Carrie and his young stepbrother were there, living with wealthy relatives. Washington was not only the capital of the United States, it was also the capital of the 'blue vein society', a term that refers to black people so light-skinned that when you looked at their inner wrists where the skin is thin, you could see their blue blood.

Langston despised intra-racial colour prejudice, he thought it was a kind of madness. He hated the fashion for light skin and for bleaching cream, crazes that soared in the 1920s. He saw his own mother humiliated in the home of her relatives because her skin was a little too brown for their tastes. He could not believe the way that dark-skinned people suffered on the streets and in the workplaces of the deeply and innately Southern city of Washington DC. And the fact they were also shunned by lighter-skinned black people as well was too much for him to bear.

Even though Langston was photographed by the great photographers of the day because he fitted the beauty ideal – light skin and wavy hair – (Carl Van Vechten's iconic portrait is one of the most well known) – Langston tried as best he could to avoid the whole scene of 'colored beauty' and the cult of the exotic. He wrote, at twenty-four, an essay that is considered part of the canon of the African diaspora, 'The Negro Artist and the Racial Mountain', published in 1926. In this essay he writes that its purpose is 'to express our individual dark-skinned selves'. He meant it. He never wanted to be white, never wanted to be light-skinned. He always regretted that he was not dark-skinned enough: 'The younger Negro artists who create now intend to express our individual dark-skinned selves without fear or shame. If white people are pleased we are glad. If they are not, it doesn't matter. We know we are beautiful. And ugly, too. The tom-tom cries, and the tom-tom laughs. If colored people are pleased we are glad. If they are not, their displeasure doesn't matter either. We build our temples for tomorrow, strong as we know how, and we stand on top of the mountain free within ourselves.'*

Along with the obsession for light skin, came 'passing' or living as a white person. The African American novelist Nella Larsen, the daughter of a Danish woman and a West Indian father, published a novel at the end of the 1920s called *Passing*, which has grown in stature over the decades as an important American work. Its subject is a black woman living as a white

---

* From 'The Negro Artist and the Racial Mountain'. Published in the *Nation* in 1926.

woman who is 'outed' by a childhood friend, and by her own inner self.

In the DC of Langston's young adulthood, there was plenty of that going around. Those who couldn't 'pass' built exclusive resorts like Idlewild in Michigan, known as the 'Black Eden'. Madame C. J. Walker, who invented a way for black women to straighten their hair, and who is mentioned in the Guinness Book of Records as the first black woman in history to be a self-made millionaire, had a home in Idlewild, as did Dr Daniel Hale Williams, the black surgeon who became the first doctor to perform open heart surgery. Some said that Idlewild referred to idle men and wild women. But beneath the 'Roaring Twenties' wild and free surface, the times were about rigid exclusivity and black people practised it, too.

Langston detested the black bourgeoisie. To get away from them, he escaped to the storefront churches, to the blues and jazz joints of the black community. His poem 'Song to a Negro Washwoman' did not amuse his snooty Washington relatives. He and his mother and stepbrother moved away from them and into a two-room apartment with no heating. It was the best they could do.

Langston could not find enough work in segregated Washington to save for university. He had to leave town, keep moving again. A few years later, after submitting a constant stream of articles and essays for publication, Langston had made his name. He was only twenty-five. Out of the huge output that he created at the time, there are three works that stand out.

In addition to 'The Negro Speaks of Rivers', there was published, in 1926, a poetry collection called *The Weary Blues*. It received immediate acclaim. Then in 1927, came another collection: *Fine Clothes to the Jew*. This received another kind of attention.

Carl Van Vechten, a white patron of the Harlem Renaissance who could do so much to make or break black careers wrote to Langston in 1926: 'My news is this: that I handed *The Weary Blues* to Knopf yesterday with the proper incantations. I do not feel particularly dubious about the outcome: your poems are too beautiful to escape appreciation. I find they have a subtle haunting quality which lingers in the memory and an extraordinary sensitivity to all that is kind and lovely.'

Droning a drowsy syncopated tune,
Rocking back and forth to a mellow croon,
I heard a Negro play.
Down on Lenox Avenue the other night
By the pale dull pallor of an old gas light
He did a lazy sway ....
He did a lazy sway ....
To the tune o' those Weary Blues.

The Weary Blues was beautiful, but the book fitted in with the tenor of the times. It also fitted in with the blues itself, and the very image of the great blues queens like Ma Rainey and Bessie Smith, big-voiced and big-hearted women who sang the way they wanted and lived the way they wanted. The intense, dolorous tones of Robert Johnson that went on to underpin rock and roll did not come into fashion until the thirties. In the twenties the blues was raucous and female.

Later that same year Langston was awarded the Witter Bynner prize for the best work written by an undergraduate, given by Lincoln University, which by then he was attending. He also won the Amy Spingarn Award, the most prestigious prize at the time that a black writer could be awarded. The time that he had devoted as a child and as a student to poetry was now paying off. As a teen, he had constantly sent work to the *Crisis* magazine and to the *Brownies' Book*; worked on the staff of his high school journal. Worked, worked, worked. All the time, he had been honing his craft, learning what mattered to him, developing his voice, coming to trust when the poems came and know in his own mind and his own heart and his own gut when they were good enough to show.

The *Crisis* planned to devote an entire page to his work, a great honour from a respected and widely read journal that campaigned for justice for black people and was hugely influential everywhere.

The *New York Herald Tribune* reported in 1926: 'Langston Hughes, although only twenty-four years old, is already conspicuous in the group of Negro intellectuals who are dignifying Harlem with a genuine art life. ... It is, however, as an individual poet, not as a member of a new and interesting literary group, or as a spokesman for a race that Langston Hughes must stand or fall. ... Always intensely subjective, passionate, keenly sensitive to beauty and possessed of an unfaltering musical sense, Langston Hughes has given us a "first book" that marks the opening of a career well worth watching.'

Alain Locke cited 'Youth', one of Langston's poems, as an example of that new spirit which Langston exemplified: 'Bright before us/Like a flame.'

In addition, Locke had included Langston in his anthology of fiction, poetry and essays entitled *The New Negro: An Interpretation*, in 1925.

It was such a magic time that Langston was even beginning to physically resemble his seventeenth-century English relative, John Quarles. The lower half of their faces were becoming the same.

The critics and the publishers wanted more of what had gone before, but Langston was moving away from the style of poetry that they liked in work such as the *The Weary Blues*. When much of black poetry was turning inward, becoming more esoteric and precious, Langston was bursting out, moving closer and closer to the street, to voices of real black people, closer to their real lives and concerns. He was reading Walt Whitman and Carl Sandburg. He wanted his poetry to address the story of black people with the same directness that they used.

Walt Whitman, a nurse during the Civil War, changed the direction of American poetry. Along with Emily Dickinson, arguably the greatest female voice in English language poetry, Whitman forged living experience into a personal expression of his inner life: his mind, his eye and his soul. Whitman's influence can be seen in Langston's 'Rivers'.

Walt Whitman's *Leaves of Grass* contained a poem which was on the surface about the assassination of Abraham Lincoln, 'When Lilacs Last in the Dooryard Bloom'd'. But it also captures something deeply personal, private and mysterious, as all great poems do. Its soaring beauty and emotional reach, its power and longing and remorse perfectly capture the sense of a nation war-weary and in shock, full of mourning and regret at the murder of a great man.

When lilacs last in the dooryard bloom'd,
And the great star early droop'd in the western sky in
the night,
I mourn'd, and yet shall mourn with ever-returning
spring.
Ever-returning spring, trinity sure to me you bring,

Lilac blooming perennial and drooping star in the
west,
And thought of him I love.

Langston also wanted to emulate the poetry of Carl Sandburg, be an 'engaged' poet, an activist, as Sandburg was. Sandburg inspired Langston's second collection of poetry, *Fine Clothes to the Jew*, published in January 1927. It shows his move towards Carl Sandburg's poet-as-activist. The title literally referred to the fact that the pawnshops in Harlem were run by mostly Jewish proprietors, and they were, in fact, the only people willing to give black people money. The term 'fine clothes to the Jew' was a 'street' expression of the time. It meant being down to your last penny, so low that you have to pawn your best clothes to the only person who has any money in Harlem, 'the Jew', or more specifically 'the white man', which was the real meaning of the term. Jewish people were by and large the only white people that most Harlemites came into contact with uptown. 'Jew' meant 'white folks' and for most African Americans, it meant no more than that.

But this definition of 'fine clothes to the Jew' is deep, inside knowledge. In other words, you have to know this. To someone with no knowledge of Harlem street jargon and especially when that title is given to a book in an era when open, rampant anti-Semitism was epidemic, the title is unfortunate to say the very least. There is no getting away from the fact that anti-Semitism was rife in American life and literature at the time. Ernest Hemingway had referred to one of the characters in his masterpiece *Fiesta*, published in the twenties, as a 'Jew', and it was not meant to be a compliment. Langston's title does play into a dangerous stereotype that ultimately had genocidal consequences for millions of innocent people.

But Langston Hughes was no anti-Semite. He was only trying to nail a reality that he heard on the streets of Harlem. The expression was an example of his aim to be 'real', to be true. In his way, he was trying to be 'street'. He meant no offence.

The critics were scathing about *Fine Clothes*.

Langston's sales plummeted. There were those who just couldn't – and wouldn't – get past the title. But the title wasn't the only problem with the book. The poems themselves were considered to be 'un-poetic'. Most of them were written in street speech. Many of them borrowed words and phrases directly from the blues. But Langston wanted to show the reality of urban life, of a life that a rural people were forging, a people not always able to leave the memories of the South behind. *Fine Clothes* is not the bright, happy lights of Harlem. Langston saw the life depicted in his poems, even as he supped at the high tables of the Harlem Renaissance and its patrons. Langston was trying to be real, trying to be true to the people. But there were segments of the African American community who found them too close to the bone, too much airing of dirty laundry, too bleak, too downbeat. Like 'Song for a Dark Girl' and 'Po' Boy Blues':

Way Down South in Dixie
(Break the heart of me)
They hung my black young lover
To a cross roads tree.
Way Down South in Dixie
(Bruised body high in air)
I asked the white Lord Jesus
What was the use of prayer.
Way Down South in Dixie
(Break the heart of me)
Love is a naked shadow
On a gnarled and naked tree.

'Po' Boy Blues'
When I was home de
Sunshine seemed like gold.
When I was home de
Sunshine seemed like gold.
Since I come up North de
Whole damn world's turned cold

What a difference a year made!
Almost a year earlier, Alfred A. Knopf had

published *The Weary Blues* to a gratifying level of acclaim. It was what people wanted, something beautiful but not challenging. *Fine Clothes* not only had a bad title, it was also considered un-Langston. Sales of the book would always remain among the lowest of all of Langston's publications.

Yet the poet had done something unique and extraordinary. He had re-drawn the emotional landscape of black life, situating the centre of the African American soul away from the idealised pastoral setting that had become all too common and placed it onto the hard, neon-lit streets of the North. He had taken African America, through his poetry, to a kind of 'Ohio'. He had honoured the Langston legacy. While this 'North' of his writing was full of dangers, it was not the plantation. It was not the South. Langston's recalibration of black life was as important as the massive change that moving to the real Ohio had been for his grandfather and grand-uncle almost a hundred years earlier. Langston was pointing the way for other black poets to follow. He was one of the first to honour black urban life.

But he was going against the trend: black people existed to provide joy and the good times. The twenties insisted on this.

One of the reasons for this attitude was the catastrophe that was World War I. Europeans and their cousins all over the world faced the end of their way of life. Certainty was gone forever, that golden summer of imperial control before the war was over. Life was suddenly unpredictable, ugly and the world seemed old. People of African descent were looked on as 'new', innocent of the old certainties that had collapsed. They were symbols of the city, of speed, of mindless fun with no consequences, of that heavy old God up in the sky who seemed to have closed His door on human beings.

In Paris, Josephine Baker, a girl considered too skinny by the black revue that had hired her to dance, and which instead cast her as 'the comedy chorus girl' who could cross her eyes and do the splits at the same time, became a sensation. Josephine danced practically in the nude; she posed in the nude; she allowed herself to be painted and sculpted in the nude; she walked down the Champs Elysées with a hint that she might not be wearing anything under her fur coat, dragging a leopard called 'Chiquita' on a lead. She had a great act, one that every African American woman living in Paris has had to live up to, or live down. Even to this day. Josephine Baker still can't be ignored. Hers is the most famous black female image of all time and no wonder.

In Harlem, Carl Van Vechten, white patron of black arts and court photographer, was so overwhelmed by it all that he wrote a novel about 'uptown' and the Renaissance called *Nigger Heaven* – the name given to the upper balcony of a movie house, where, because of segregation, black people were relegated.

The majestic African American writer James Weldon Johnson gave *Nigger Heaven* a cautious but laudatory review. W.E.B DuBois considered it an affront to 'black hospitality and white intelligence'. Langston noted that more black people bought that book than bought books by all of the black authors of the Renaissance combined.

Zora Neale Hurston, the raucous Florida genius, hit Harlem running. She was witty and a player. Her short story 'Spunk' was selected for Locke's *The New Negro*. She soon joined a group of writers and artists who adopted for themselves black writer Wallace Thurman's satirical and provocative name: the 'Niggerati'. The Niggerati re-fashioned the most pejorative term that could be hurled at an African American to suit themselves and included in their gang anyone who wanted to break boundaries – in every way. They published a literary magazine called *Fire!!* which Langston said was named that way because it wanted to burn down everything old. But some in the black community thought that the magazine contained too much fire and did not show African Americans in a dignified and positive light. Most of the young black people associated with *Fire!!* did not really care what the black community thought since the black community did not buy the magazine anyway. As far as they were concerned, *Fire!!* set out to break new ground, so all 'old school' criticism was a good thing.

That rebellious spirit quietened down during the Depression.

Part of the spirit of rebellion that was *Fire!!* was its acceptance and celebration of homosexuality. It is now generally accepted and respected that Langston Hughes was a closet homosexual. To have 'come out' would have risked becoming a victim of the homophobia and hatred of elements of the black community, with horrible consequences for his poetry, even for his life. At the very least, he would have been shunned, ostracised, his work denounced from the churches, untouched by the schools, left unread, the fate of many black homosexual, lesbian and transgender artists and poets even today. The odds are that Langston would have been excised from the community. Above all else, Langston could not have taken that. And so, like many before and after him, Langston kept a critical part of himself hidden for all of his life. We will never know what price he paid for doing this. As a black man. As a poet. As a human being.

Today Langston Hughes is celebrated as a gay icon and more and more information about his life is coming to light.

Langston's patron, Charlotte Mason, however, only cared about him as a writer. Her kind of writer.

Widow of a millionaire, she funded him, making it possible for him to write, especially his first novel. But her interest was in 'primitive' peoples, and when Langston stopped writing the way she liked she withdrew her support, devastating him. She is responsible, however, for the completion of his first novel *Not Without Laughter* which he published at the beginning of the next decade.

Laughter is a novel of character development instead of the 'primitivism' that Mason preferred. Langston writes about the main character's 'awakening to the sad and the beautiful realities of black life in a small Kansas town'. There is none of the exoticism that his patron craved. This was the Kansas life that he knew very well. He had lived it.

By the end of the twenties, Langston, too, was in his late twenties and he had had enough. He had had enough of the feuds and the fawning, the literature and the lies, the noise, the glitz, the bathtub booze that could kill or worse, all mixed with a tonic ironically called Canada Dry. Then the stock market bubble burst, causing the Wall Street Crash in 1929. And it was all change.

All change for Langston, too. He had moved on. He knew that he was risking the loss of patronage, awards, accolades, attention, but the black working class – ordinary people – were the ones he wanted to write about. He wanted to live out the freedom and perhaps the melancholy and irony of what he had written in 'Dream Variations' onboard a ship heading for Africa.

To fling my arms wide
In some place of the sun
To whirl and to dance
Till the white day is done.

He was entering a new life. He could never have guessed how far it would lead.

CHAPTER SEVEN

LANGSTON FINALLY GRADUATED from Lincoln University, a black university in Pennsylvania in 1929.

But at the same time he entered into a deep depression when he realised that Charlotte Mason, who had supported him while writing his first novel, had backed away from supporting him any further. She had praised him to the skies and now, because he was changing direction – growing – told him that she could no longer do so. She had been like a godmother to him. But he no longer wanted to create work like his privately printed poetry collection *Dear Lovely Death* which seemed to speak only to him and other elites; nor was he interested in pleasing those in the black community who only wanted to read 'uplift'.

At the end of the twenties and beginning of the thirties, he was going somewhere else. It was what he wanted after his experience at Columbia, and in the Harlem of the Renaissance. *Not Without Laughter* took him back to his days in Kansas as a lonely child full of longing. He dug deep down to find the things that marked that experience, things that made it a black experience. He wanted to paint a portrait, let people *see* as well as feel what he knew and what he meant.

Little did he know, as he worked, that his attempts to forge a kind of black consciousness would inspire so many other black writers around the world: francophone writers, titans of French literature Nicolás Guillén, Jacques Roumain; Léopold Sédar Senghor from Africa, and the Caribbean writers Aimé Césaire, René Maran and Léon Damas among others. He helped to inspire the creation of the Négritude movement in their French-speaking black world which sought to reshape black identity and to expand and deepen French literature in the face of colonialism. Langston did not know of these writers at the time, could not have known how important they would become, and how much they owed to him. All that he knew after Charlotte Mason dropped him was that he had to keep working. He agreed to write a play with one of his Harlem Renaissance friends, the writer Zora Neale Hurston.

Zora did anthropology studies among the black people of her native Eatonville in Florida, partly work for her white patrons that allowed the wily writer to do her own work. She is the master of African American rural Florida speech. Her novels, short stories, her collection and preservation for all time of some of the most beautiful and powerful sermons and speeches have made her world-famous. She came to her friend Langston with an idea for a play called *Mule Bone* and they decided to work together. *Mule Bone* tells the story of two black men: one a Baptist and the other a Methodist, who fall out over a woman and as a result one hits the other over the head with a bone from a mule. There is a kind of trial in a bar and it all revolves around whether a mule bone is a weapon. It probably sounded delightful and funny when Zora told Langston the story, probably something she was told by an Eatonville resident during one of her anthropological trips, but actually writing it down as a play turned out to be disastrous. There are accounts of Zora vanishing, and returning to try to claim sole authorship. There was too much Harlem Renaissance madness about Zora. Langston couldn't go back to that. They would always love one another, but he had to give it up. Besides, the rumour was that since Charlotte Mason was also Zora's patron, Zora didn't want Langston to rub off on her and cause Mason to drop her, too. Langston put a note on the script: 'This play was never done because the authors fell out'. It was finally performed on Broadway about twenty years ago, and the critics agreed that perhaps Langston and Zora should have finished it before it was produced.

But their personal drama was nothing compared with the catastrophe that was happening in the world. There are many, many theories as to why the world began to collapse in the autumn of 1929: the fact that the population was so low after the Great War of 1914–1918; the flu pandemic of 1918 that had killed almost more people than the war; even theories like the rise of secularism which meant that people did not start families; and other theories like credit being too easy; protectionism; the war reparations; the gold standard, and on and on. Whatever the reason, the world's economic system collapsed, and it hit farmers and miners the hardest. As well as racial segregation, black people now had to face starvation. Afterwards they helped build shanty towns known as 'Hoovervilles' after President Hoover, whom everybody blamed for the mess.

Beautiful, literary poems no longer expressed the lives of ordinary people, nor served them. They did not express what Langston wanted to say, either.

In 1931 he published the poetry collection *The Negro Mother and Other Dramatic Recitations*. He had to give voice to what he was seeing, to what he knew:

Children, I come back today
To tell you a story of the long dark way
That I had to climb, that I had to know

In order that the race might live and grow.
[...]
Oh, my dark children, may my dreams and my prayers
Impel you forever up the great stairs –
For I will be with you till no white brother
Dares keep down the children of the Negro Mother.

He was writing poems now that demanded to be recited aloud in huge halls, to crowds of people ready to change the world.

The Communist Party USA was ready to answer the call. It is important to understand how a person fighting for justice, for equality, in the 1930s would have seen the Communist Party. As the Depression deepened, people turned to political explanations for it and then wanted political solutions. Capitalism seemed to be not only the source of the catastrophe, but it itself also seemed to have collapsed. There appeared to be several answers. There was the fascist solution: Germany and Italy had chosen it and Spain was in turmoil because of it. And there was the solution presented by communism.

For many Americans, communism made sense because it saw the world situation as a result of the class struggle. All over the world, for intellectuals and workers alike, there was only one answer: communism must take over the world. In England, five young students decided to work for the Soviet Union.

The 'Cambridge Five' became a part of the British Establishment while spying for Russia. They never repented, considering the Establishment part of the problem, a problem that needed to be overthrown by what communism called the 'proletariat' – the worker, the peasant, the ordinary person.

There was one event during the Depression, which caused all black people to rise up in protest and made the Communist Party, for many, the only defender of justice.

On 25 March 1931, in Scottsboro, Alabama, nine young black men, hitching a ride on a train, got into a fight with a group of white men onboard. When the train stopped they were arrested for assault. Then the police discovered that two white women had also been in the same railroad car. The police automatically accused the black men of rape, and threw them in jail, an open invitation to the local Klan to drag them out of their cells and lynch them. A campaign to save the 'Scottsboro Boys' was born. The Communist Party's legal defence organisation leapt into action, sending their lawyers and activists down South. They worked with the men and their families. In Harlem, unofficial capital of African America, the Communist Party became famous for its total, unhesitating commitment to this cause. The sight of white people fighting in the street, taking on the police, all on behalf of black people, was new and overwhelming. And empowering.

Communism enthralled many black communities, especially Harlem, because of the Scottsboro case. The Depression in general had aroused a new militancy in Harlem that led to campaigns like 'Don't Buy Where You Can't Work', a successful initiative to force businesses to hire black people. A riot that broke out in 1935 in which 600 stores were looted and burned and three men died had communist support. When Ethiopia was invaded by Italy, Harlemites came together in a new international solidarity. Some of this activity happened with the help of the Soviet Union's organisation set up to foster revolution outside of the Soviet Union: the Comintern.

A number of prominent African Americans aligned themselves to the Party.

In 1933, Adam Clayton Powell, Jr., the leading preacher in Harlem stated: 'I don't mind being called a communist ... the day will come when being called a communist will be the highest honour that can be paid an individual and that day is coming soon.'

Duke Ellington, Dizzy Gillespie and Billie Holiday, titans from the world of jazz, and Countee Cullen, Ralph Ellison and Langston, too, from the world of literature, plus dozens of other prominent black people, stood up for the Party at some point in their lives because of the Scottsboro Boys. It was completely logical.

Langston himself went to the Soviet Union in 1932–33, and the trip inspired him to write some of his most radical verse including: *Scottsboro Limited: Four Poems and a Play*, which included the infamous 'Christ in Alabama':

> *Christ is a Nigger,*
> *Beaten and black —*
> *O, bare your back...*
> *Most holy bastard*
> *Of the bleeding mouth:*
> *Nigger Christ*
> *On the cross of the South.*

He also wrote *A Negro Looks at Soviet Central Asia*. Because of his passionate political commitment on behalf of African Americans and the poor and oppressed everywhere and the effect that it had on his work, some critics, especially in America, consider Langston's work from the thirties to be mediocre. But many of these critics are politically conservative and are condemning his work from this time on an ideological political basis. It is true that Langston was involved with organisations linked to the Communist Party, some of them 'front organisations' in which connections to the Party were hidden. It is not known whether he was actually a member of the CPUSA, which was not then and is not now illegal in the States. But he did lend his name to many of these 'fronts': the John Reed Clubs; the League of Struggle for Negro Rights; the National Negro Congress; the League of Professional Groups for Foster and Ford; the League of American Writers. He supported the Soviet Union, even in public, and did not denounce the purges of 'counter-revolutionaries' carried out by Stalin in 1938.

His critics point to poems like 'New Song' to condemn his politics:

I speak in the name of the black millions
Awakening to action.
Let all others keep silent a moment
I have this word to bring,
This thing to say,
This song to sing.

Langston could not know that this and other poems and writings would be used to try and destroy him. And no one could foresee that the government programmes that he participated in which helped the poor would come to be seen by many as examples of communist subversion.

In an effort to stimulate the economy, President Franklin Roosevelt initiated an economic stimulus programme called the Works Project Administration. Under this initiative, Federal Project Number One was created, which contained five sub-programmes: Federal Writers' Project (FWP); Historical

Records Survey (HRS, originally part of the FWP); Federal Theater Project (FTP); Federal Music Project (FMP); Federal Art Project (FAP).

The FWP was the largest project. It compiled histories, ethnographies, children's books, oral histories. One of the most beautiful and important oral histories to emerge from the FWP was 'Slave Narratives from the Federal Writers' Project, 1936–1938' which contains over 2,300 first-person accounts of the enslaved and 500 black-and-white photos of former slaves. It exists online today, the result of a government programme to create jobs.

Langston was employed under the FWP (he did not work on the slave narratives). Ralph Ellison, who went on to write the classic fifties novel of black alienation, *Invisible Man*, and to reject his 'leftist' past, was also employed under the FWP. Richard Wright was helped by the Chicago branch of the FWP.

Langston's poetry, short stories, recitations, novels and other writing continued at full throttle. He wrote *The Ways of White Folks*, a forensic examination of African American life; and a children's book, with his friend, the African American writer Arna Bontemps, who resembled Langston. Arna, too, had also had the obligatory Carl Van Vechten photo taken against a backdrop of drapes complete with moody lighting and wistful gaze. Langston had met Bontemps, from Louisiana, during the Harlem Renaissance, and in the thirties they collaborated on a children's book called *Popo and Fifina*. The book is a landmark in children's literature. It is important because Langston and Arna take a working-class black Haitian family and render them as people recognisable to Western children; they tell the story of their everyday lives. They don't glorify it, condemn it or excuse it; just present it. The book was a triumph partly because Americans during the Depression era could better relate to the lives of ordinary Haitians than they can today.

There was also a poetry collection for children published in 1932, the same year as *Popo and Fifina*, called *The Dream Keeper and Other Poems*. This was charming and sweet stuff, in contrast to Langston's poetry for adults which became more and more political.

'Let America Be America Again' contained these lines:

I am the poor white, fooled and pushed apart,
I am the Negro bearing slavery's scars.
I am the red man driven from the land,
I am the immigrant clutching the hope I seek –
And finding only the same old stupid plan
Of dog eat dog, of mighty crush the weak.

Black theatre thrived under the federal stimulus plan, although black theatre professionals had to take to the streets and protest to make the Negro Theater Project (NTP) even happen. The young twenty-year-old writer and director, Orson Welles, part of the all-white leadership of the NTP (the exception being the 'first lady of the Negro-theater' Rose McClendon who was one of the stars of Langston's *Mulatto*) made his name with his *Voodoo Macbeth*. The CPUSA condemned it before it opened but it went on to become a huge success and a great source of pride in Harlem. Legend has it that one critic who made the mistake of writing a bad review of the play found out that a cast member had made a voodoo doll of him. Welles found the doll amusing, especially after the cast member told him that he used it to curse the critic.

Shortly afterwards, the critic died.

Langston had inherited his mother Carrie's love of the theatre. Although he never acted on stage like his mother had, he considered the theatre to be one of the more perfect art forms through which to express the life of black people. He also found out that the theatre could be tricky, too.

Mulatto, the 1935 Broadway production of his play about the South, had a completely gratuitous rape scene created by his producer and added at the last minute without Langston's knowledge. Even though he won a Guggenheim Fellowship that same year, the play was so notorious in the black community that it almost destroyed Langston's reputation. But he went on to write and have produced *The Emperor of Haiti* (1936) and *Don't You Want to Be Free* (1938), a piece of political theatre which combined the blues, black nationalism and socialist exhortations. It was put on by the theatre he founded in Harlem, the Suitcase Theater, an apt name for any venture involving Langston. That same year *A New Song* was published.

Black filmmaking in the 1930s continued a long tradition that began at the very dawn of the film industry. The 1920s, led by the producer-director-writer Oscar Micheaux's 1924 film *Body and Soul*, introduced the world to Paul Robeson, one of the twentieth century's artistic and political titans.

Black and Tan Fantasy (1929) was a short film starring Duke Ellington and his orchestra, complete with the Duke even acting a role. In 1932, Micheaux wrote, directed and produced a film called *Veiled Aristocrats* about black people passing for white starring Lorenzo Tucker. Tucker, very light-skinned, had played on stage opposite the blonde bombshell Mae West whom he was supposed to kiss. The theatre patrons of Washington DC violently objected to a black man kissing a white woman so the feisty West closed the play rather than recast. Her New York producers however totally refused to even cast Lorenzo and he was replaced by a Greek-American actor who had to 'black up' for the part.

Fredi Washington, so light-skinned that her agent begged her to pass for white so that she could get more work, also suffered because of her colour, particularly in the movies. She acted opposite Paul Robeson in *The Emperor Jones*. She played a black girl who passes for white in *Imitation of Life*, which won an Oscar. As righteous as she was beautiful, Fredi went on to involve herself in the civil rights struggle. She was 'blacklisted' – shut out of work – as a result.

Matthew 'Stymie' Beard played the cute little black boy in the *Our Gang* series. A brilliant little kid, Matthew also managed to get his sister, brother and mother speaking-parts in the series, which helped support his thirteen brothers and sisters living in dire poverty in east Los Angeles. Clarence Muse was another African American film pioneer, who began as an actor in the late twenties. He and Langston wrote a film called *Way Down South*, notable because it was shot on a real farm in the South with non-professional black actors in the lead, a pioneering effort in the history of cinema. It showed black Southern life in a realistic manner for the first time. The film was a success, and Langston thought that he might be able to get more film work. But Hollywood would not be ready for a black screenwriter for many decades to come.

And this was not his only problem.

He had not only been to the Soviet Union, he

had also been to Spain visiting the left-wing Loyalists fighting against the right-wing General Franco. In addition, his writings had become more and more incendiary. None of this looked good as the times became more and more conservative. But strangely, he soon found himself the target not of political conservatives, but of the growing evangelism that had begun in America shortly after World War I. Protestant revivalism has always been a part of American culture. After the war, it grew quickly, helped by the rise of new technology like the radio. The novelist Sinclair Lewis wrote a satirical novel called *Elmer Gantry* about a con man turned preacher. In the thirties, a Roman Catholic priest by the name of Father Coglin used his radio broadcast to spew anti-Semitic hate speech and preach what amounted to fascism.

But it was a Canadian tent preacher by the name of Aimee Semple McPherson who, with a savvy use of the new technology combined with a prairie sex appeal and great charisma, changed the face of religion and politics, too. She made little sense but spoke in such 'down home' tones that it did not matter. Thousands came to her Sunday services and millions listened to her rants on radio. She was so powerful that she helped to turn the country to the right, causing President Roosevelt's stimulus programme, the New Deal, to be waylaid by a new conservative Congress in 1937. The rollback of the New Deal helped to cause a recession which was only lifted by World War II. The conservatives then demanded that the government stop spending. McPherson preached that this was the will of God. Langston and writers like him became caught up in a reactionary wave against those who wrote about American injustice, and who happened to benefit from programmes paid for by the federal government.

Langston kept writing, like most people not seeing the warning signs. He did not comprehend what the conservative win in Congress actually meant for people like him. By 1939, both of his parents, Carrie and James Nathaniel were dead. In many ways, Langston had always been his own mother and father and now he truly was.

War was on the horizon and he had said that black people should not fight, a stance he later repudiated, but nevertheless it had been said.

In spite of the pressure he was starting to feel from political forces opposed to him, Langston felt a small glimmer of hope. His writing career was continuing at a great pace, and he was convinced that he could crack Hollywood if he just kept going like he always did. It seemed that all of the marches and speeches and uprisings and writings that he and those like him had done were starting to bear fruit.

Marian Anderson, a celebrated African American contralto who had sung throughout Europe, had wanted to perform at Constitution Hall in Washington DC. But the Daughters of the American Revolution (DAR), an ultra elite group of descendants (all white at the time) of those who had fought in the American Revolution, refused to allow her to perform in front of an integrated audience. Eleanor Roosevelt, the First Lady, resigned from the DAR in protest. She and the President made it possible for Miss Anderson to perform on the steps of a more symbolic place: the Lincoln Memorial.

Today the DAR's racist past is behind them. There are several black members of the organisation, some even descended directly from the Founding Fathers. But it was the stand taken by Eleanor Roosevelt in 1939 that made headlines around the world. When Germany invaded Poland, starting World War II, the September after Marian Anderson's triumph, Langston thought that it might be possible now for all Americans to come together as a beacon for the free world.

He entered the next decade a famous and popular writer. He was also considered an artist, part of the American literary canon. He was still anxious about money, still anxious to get the story of his people right, but he had demonstrated his versatility and his ability to survive. James Nathaniel Hughes had been proven wrong once and for all. A black man could make it in America by the strength of his pen. He,

James Mercer Langston Hughes could make it. He was making it.

The coming war would show America what black people were really made of, he had no doubt.

At the end of the 1930s, Langston looked forward to the future with some optimism, and for the first time, with a sense of personal security. He was about to publish his autobiography. He knew that it would do well.

But the next decade would bring a political force which would use his past to try and make everything his life had stood for mean nothing.

CHAPTER EIGHT

AT THE BEGINNING OF 1940, while much of the world was at war, the United States was providing assistance to Great Britain and the Empire, and preparing for what would inevitably come.

During 1940, A. Philip Randolph, the African American president of the campaigning group, the Brotherhood of Sleeping Car Porters – Langston too had worked as a valet on the trains – threatened to march on Washington, protesting the conditions of working black people. President Roosevelt, a champion of the rights of African American people, nonetheless signed an Executive Order to stop the march. War was coming. The next march on Washington on behalf of jobs and equality for black people would not take place until twenty-three years later under the leadership of Martin Luther King Jr.

In the North, black people were, for the most part, relegated to ghettos, police states where any possibility of mobility and escape were virtually impossible.

This ghettoisation is one of the reasons that many African American voices have a Southern intonation, a result of our isolation from other accents, other ways of speaking.

By 1940, Langston was now a famous American writer, the most famous black writer who had ever lived. He had pulled himself up to that level by his genius, his talent, by patronage, luck, sheer self-belief and a refusal to give up on his writing. Turning everything he could into words, he had helped forge an identity for his people, and not only African Americans, but all those who were marginalised and oppressed. He had created the gold standard and anyone even attempting to write about being non-white in a white world had to look to Langston to understand how to do it.

He was still struggling to make enough money to have the kind of life a white writer of his stature had, but he understood who and what he was in the land of his birth. The irony of the Declaration of Independence and the US Constitution in relation to black people never left him, and he aimed to make that irony and contradiction visible to all. He wanted to do this particularly for black people; because that irony could serve as a source of comfort, a place to go when nothing made sense at all.

In 1940 he published his autobiography, *The Big Sea*.

The 'big sea' was life itself, and many other things as well. He took his peripatetic childhood and turned it into a kind of lyrical magic. He was passionate about rendering black life beautiful in and of itself, and to show black people as worthy and capable of survival. Black speech to him was rich and complex, alive with hidden meaning. But it was always at its best, as far as Langston was concerned, when it was beautiful and humorous.

For him, beauty and humour were the marks of a brave, majestic people. To be downtrodden and unhappy in the face of misery is beneath the majestic spirit of African people. Langston's goal always is to show that black people are at their best when they are direct, plain-spoken and with no airs and graces.

'When I was in the second grade, my grandmother took me to Lawrence to raise me. And I was unhappy for a long time, and very lonesome, living with my grandmother. Then it was that books began to happen to me, and I began to believe in nothing but books and the wonderful world in books – whcrc if people suffered, they suffered in beautiful language, not in monosyllables, as we did in Kansas.' With these words Langston shows himself to be still very much a part of the modernism of the Harlem Renaissance. His combination of lyrical writing and a kind of brutal reportage was very much in the style of Hemingway and F. Scott Fitzgerald, too. But Langston combines them here in his own way, while revealing an experience that they could never know.

The Big Sea had made him more popular than ever, but he sensed the coming events. Like the great pre-war German expressionist painters who had *felt* World War I coming and had responded by making paintings of brutal reality, Langston could see the coming apocalypse reflected on the streets of New York City, in Harlem, where he had finally made a permanent place for himself after decades of wandering. He wrote about how New York had begun to change in the run-up to war, that it had become more unpleasant.

When the Japanese Imperial Airforce launched a sneak attack on the US Naval Base at Pearl Harbor, Hawaii, on the sleepy Sunday morning of 7 December 1941, the US finally entered World War II. The Japanese Airforce effectively destroyed the US Pacific Fleet, killing over a thousand people, and causing President Roosevelt to declare 7 December 1941 'a day of infamy'.

Almost overnight, the mighty American industrial war machine went into overdrive. African Americans stepped up to the plate, joining the war effort to bring their nation to victory. Langston watched a new generation of African American men and women join the fight against fascism. Over 2.5 million African American men registered for the draft and thousands of black women volunteered. What they met with – even during war-time – was the old enemy: racial segregation. Yet there was great heroism in spite of this.

On 7 December 1941, during the attack on Pearl Harbor, mess attendant Doris 'Dorie' Miller came to the aid of his shipmates on the USS *West Virginia*. He helped to move the wounded away from the line of fire, and aided his dying superior officer. He took control of an anti-aircraft gun, although he had no training on it, taking down several Japanese aircraft. Dorie won the Navy Cross, the first black serviceman to be given this honour. That black men could only be messmen – the job Langston took whenever he worked on ships, and the job one of my own late uncles was restricted to in World War II – makes this award even more remarkable. Dorie Miller was killed in action in 1943, and in the Navy he is still a legend. Yet for every story of the respect shown to black servicemen and women, there were stories like the one about German prisoners of war given better rations than black serving men, until the black men revolted at one camp and things changed fast.

The US Marine Corps began enlisting African Americans in 1942 for the first time. General Benjamin O. Davis Sr, the first black general in the American military, a graduate of West Point, commanded the corps of black airmen called the Tuskegee

Airmen. They were only allowed to train en masse at one airfield in the country, the one called Tuskegee. Black female nurses were often housed close to white servicemen's quarters, in complete disrespect for the women's gender, leaving them subject to sexual assault and violence.

But they continued to serve their country.

Langston had said once that black people should not serve in the military because of racial segregation at home and in the very armed services itself. He repudiated his position both in word and deed but he knew that African America had had enough. In Harlem, in particular, the teachings and example of Marcus Garvey underpinned the anger of the people.

Marcus Mosiah Garvey, Jr, now designated a 'National Hero Of Jamaica', was a Pan-Africanist, Black Nationalist, journalist, publisher and entre-preneur, who advocated a doctrine called African Redemption, as a means to create a worldwide move-ment to take Africa back from European domina-tion and to put black people all over the world 'on their feet'. He wrote: 'Our union must know no clime, boundary, or nationality ...'

In racist, segregated America, Garvey eventu-ally became Public Enemy Number One. Garvey lived in London from 1912–14, where he worked for black newspapers, attended Birkbeck College, and often spoke at Speakers' Corner in Hyde Park.

He co-founded the Universal Negro Improvement Association (UNIA) in Jamaica in August 1914, the month that World War I was declared. He came to the US in 1916, after corresponding with the African American educator and leader Booker T. Washington, who would have approved of his doctrine of black self-help.

During World War I, Garvey spoke on street corners in Harlem, making a speaking tour of the country, promoting black economic and political freedom. In time he created a fleet called the Black Star Line. He held a convention in New York, speaking to almost 30,000 people. He was responsible for the creation of black-owned industries, advocated a union of black businesses in the States, Central and South America, the Caribbean and Africa, in addition to developing Liberia as a permanent home for black people. Garvey was also controversial for meeting with the Ku Klux Klan and stating that they were more honest than most white people. Several African American leaders came out against him because of this.

The agency that was forerunner to the FBI hired its first black agents in order to dig up something on Garvey. A false accusation of mail fraud was created, Garvey stood trial, lost, was sentenced and jailed. In federal prison in Atlanta he wrote his famous 'First Message to the Negroes of the World from Atlanta

Prison': 'Look for me in the whirlwind ... look for me all around you, for, with God's grace, I shall come and bring with me countless millions of black slaves who have died in America and the West Indies and the millions in Africa to aid you in the fight for Liberty, Freedom and Life.'

On his release, Garvey travelled to the League of Nations, the world organisation that existed before the UN, to put the black case before the world body. By 1937, after spending time in Jamaica, he returned to London where he supported the cause of Ethiopia against the Italian invasion, making him, today, a hero of the Rastafarians. In London he had two strokes. The second, some say, killed him after he had read in the leading African American newspaper in Chicago, the *Defender*, that he had died from the first stroke 'broke, alone, and unpopular'.

Today Marcus Garvey is immortal all over the black world, even in Chicago. The Nation of Islam, known as the Black Muslims, whose power centre is Chicago, uses the philosophy of black self-help that Garvey extolled. The great African nationalist leader Kwame Nkrumah named the national football team of Ghana 'Black Stars' after Garvey's fleet of ships: The Black Star Line.

Garvey deserves an extensive explanation because both he and his philosophy were one of the dominant theories running counter to the idea of integration, and the stance of 'be patient and wait'. Young people, in particular, invoked Garvey during the Harlem riot that started on 1 August 1943, when a black soldier was shot and the rumour spread that he had been killed by a white policeman. Two days later, six people were dead, hundreds wounded, and millions of dollars worth of property destroyed. Harlemites, although they were part of the electoral structure of New York, were tired of its racism. It was whites who rioted when homes were offered to black people in Detroit in 1942, and by 1943 the atmosphere was so volatile there that when a black man and a white man started fighting at an amusement park, a huge race riot broke out, ending days later when the President sent in federal troops to quell the violence. All of this took place during World War II.

And Langston kept writing, working at an even more frantic pace, attempting to understand and interpret what was going on around him, trying to stay true to what was inside of him, what he knew. But events were outpacing him. He was becoming subsumed in the tide of history.

By 1944, the use of armed black soldiers on the front line had become reality. Before that, they had not been allowed to carry guns except during special circumstances. Black men were mainly used as support. They cooked, served as servants, did chores, drove supply trucks. One of the GIs who drove a truck in the Red Ball Express, the mighty convoy manned largely by African American soldiers which kept the front supplied after D-Day, was my father, just out of his teens. He served in Europe the year before the war ended when the segregation of the United States Armed Forces *had* to break down simply because so many white soldiers had been killed.

During the last German offensive, known as the the Battle of the Bulge, black soldiers, including my dad, no longer relegated behind the lines – came into their own. President Obama's great-uncle and my father were there together, but they had a different war. Because the President's great-uncle was white. They both would have been present at the concentration camps that were liberated; they would both have served under their commander, the legendary George Patton, who had said, when warned that black men were being given guns, that he didn't care if they were green as long as they could shoot.

After all of that, some returning veterans in the South were subjected to humiliation, even murder by the Klan and other whites. In the North, whites refused to allow black veterans and their families the housing set aside for veterans who had fought for their country. Young black soldiers, like my father, had no intention of returning after the war to an America that intended to carry on with business as usual.

In Chicago, in 1946, a race riot known as the Airport Homes Race Riot, broke out, largely driven by white mums, grannies and little kids during the daytime while the men were at work. What with other race riots like the 1943 anti-Hispanic/Filipino riots in Los Angeles known as the Zoot Suit Riots – Orson Welles came out in support of the Latinos and Filipinos, his movie-star wife, Rita Hayworth was Hispanic – all Americans had to face the reality of the 'war at home'.

In 1948, the Supreme Court ruled in a case known as Shelley vs Kraemer, that no one could, under the Fourteenth Amendment, stop another American citizen from buying a house. This ruling from the highest court in the land, threw out the restrictive covenants that had kept black people from living where they wanted. This did not end those racial covenants, but it was a turning point, as was President Truman's desegregation of the armed services by Executive Order in that same year of 1948.

For Langston, running parallel to these momentous events, as always, was his work. He was more prolific during the 1940s than he had ever been. And things looked good for him. At first.

In 1940, Langston had formed the Negro Playwrights' Company in New York City with Alain Locke, his old Harlem Renaissance mentor, Paul Robeson, and the novelist Richard Wright, who was beginning to make a name for himself. Theodore Ward, another good friend and also a part of the company, had written a play, *Big White Fog*. Set in a black household in Chicago in the twenties, it was a sensation. The play showed the black community split three ways between Garveyism, communism, and the American Dream.

Langston was being torn, too, between the political and social events of the time, and his need to write. This very need was being threatened by a series of events that he could never have foreseen.

Culture itself was becoming a battleground. There a war was raging, too, and before America entered the war, the Rockefeller Commission Seminar began a study of mass communication. In that same year, Walt Disney, a fierce opponent of the Left, released an animated feature called *Pinocchio*. The film implied that amusement parks were places of subversion, one of 'Uncle Walt's' beliefs about the danger America was in from the 'red' – the communist enemy within.

In 1941, a hit film was released called *Meet John Doe*. Hidden within its amusing plot was a warning about media manipulation: in the month of Pearl Harbor *Sullivan's Travels* opened, a story about a movie director who goes underground, looking for the real America. In the same year came *Citizen Kane* the story of a right-wing newspaper mogul who owns all of the wealth in America but loses his soul. This movie is regularly considered by critics to be one of the greatest films ever made.

F. Scott Fitzgerald's last novel was published post-humously in 1941: *The Last Tycoon*, about an ideal-istic producer fighting the System. In 1942 came the painting *Nighthawk*, a bleak masterpiece depicting lonely people in a diner, people left out of the Ameri-can Dream. This painting has influenced many film directors, including the Coen Brothers. The screen idol Jimmy Cagney, an avowed conservative and on the Right, released *Yankee Doodle Dandy*, in which he brilliantly dances and sings as a celebration of the American Way. He won an Oscar for his efforts. Tennessee Williams produced his stage masterpiece *The Glass Menagerie*. The character of Tom (Tennes-see Williams' real name) goes to the movies a great deal, he sees them as liberation, escape, but in reality, movies, along with the rest of American culture were being policed, and put in a straight-jacket.

Art, high and low, was beginning to be examined for traces of communism. A new government agency, the Office of War Information was created to oversee all movies produced in Hollywood. In 1944, American conservatives and right-wingers formed the Motion Picture Alliance for the Preservation of American Ideals, to fight 'communists, radicals and crackpots'. In 1945, at the end of the war, a movie studio strike was called, said to have been started by communist subversives of the far Left. When the actor Ronald Reagan – later President of the United States – was the president of the actors union, the Screen Actors Guild, anti-communist investigations were stepped up. Certain Hollywood writers, directors and producers were called to Washington to appear before a committee of the House of Representatives, the lower house of the US Congress. These intimidating hearings, held in public with lawyers, were created to investigate communism in American life. The hearings were called by the House Un-American Activities Committee, the infamous HUAC.

Repression had begun as Hollywood and the arts were being swept clean of what was considered to be anything and anyone against the 'American Way of Life'. People lived in terror of being called to Washington. Many people worked under assumed names. Writers paid people – 'fronts' – to submit their work under the other person's name. Marriages broke down, families were destroyed; a person could find herself in work one day and cast out of her profession the next. Some went into exile. Some were trapped in the US, like Paul Robeson, unable to travel abroad to work because he had been denied a passport. Paranoia, depression, madness, suicide; these were the results of the new, post-war America.

Langston, up against the assault on the arts on one side, and the assault against racism on the other, tried to keep his head down, to do what he had always done. To survive. He worked at his usual frantic pace. His poetry had become vast and varied: *Shakespeare in Harlem* in 1942; *Fields of Wonder* in 1947; *One-Way Ticket* in 1949. He translated French and Spanish texts such as *Cuba Libre* by Nicolás Guillén, the opera *Canto de Una Muchacha Negra* by Silvestre Revueltas and *Masters of the Dew* by Jacques Roumain. He edited *The Poetry of the Negro* with his friend Arna Bontemps in 1949. There were operas, musicals and gospel plays. *The Organizer*, his first performed opera, with music by James P. Johnson, was presented at Carnegie Hall in 1940 under the auspices of a trade union.

Troubled Island, a collaboration with William Grant Still, the first African American composer in the US to have a symphony performed by a major company, and the first black man to conduct a white orchestra in the Deep South, was performed in 1949. The opera – Langston had transformed a play he had written in the thirties into a libretto – was based on the life of Jean-Jacques Dessalines, the Haitian patriot. Langston also contributed the lyrics to Kurt Weill's *Street Scene*, a landmark of the American musical theatre. The playwright Elmer Rice, who had written the play upon which the opera was based, tried to take credit for Langston's work. But he didn't get away with it. The experience was hell, but the success of the opera enabled Langston to buy a house in Harlem, which had always been his dream. This episode was one of the reasons Langston was often wary around white people. As he would say about what he saw as white exploitation of black talent: 'You've taken my blues and gone ...'

Gospel music exploded as an industry in the 1940s, and although Langston was most at home in the blues and jazz, he tried his hand at it. In *Black Nativity* he set out to dramatise gospel singing itself and bring back the religious pageant. In 1948, in one of his constant attempts to pay some bills, he created the lyrics for a musical *Just Around the Corner*, another maddening theatre experience. He wrote to Arna Bontemps warning him about the theatre, how it can not only cripple the legs, but cripple the soul, too. Nevertheless, tragedy, comedy, history, pastoral musical, he never abandoned the theatre and the theatre never abandoned him. It was just as he had said in 1931, when he won the Harmon Medal and $400, the most money he had ever seen in his life: 'Literature was a big sea where one puts down one's nets. And I'm still pulling.'

In 1943, Lincoln University awarded him an honorary Doctor of Letters. He became visiting professor of creative writing at Atlanta University in 1947 and poet in residence at the racially integrated Laboratory School of the University of Chicago in 1949. He accepted

multiple book contracts, working on them simultane-
ously, maintaining a killing work schedule. He always
kept his 'smokes' and a typewriter at the ready.

In 1942, in an attempt to get a larger audience and
a steady income, he accepted the *Defender*'s invitation to write a weekly column. His early work on it
was controversial and cantankerous, his attempt at
reacting to the week's events. Southern segregation,
collapsing colonialism, the Soviet Union, the segregated Broadway production of the play *Anna Luca-
sta*, all felt the wrath of his typewriter.

Then on 21 November 1941, he introduced a black
Everyman, a guy who spoke his mind, by the name
of Jesse B. Semple, shortened to 'Simple'. Simple is an
offbeat Harlemite, talking to a narrator called Boyd in
a Harlem bar. He talks about money, women, and life.
'White folks,' he would say, were the cause of all of the
inconvenience in his life. He was an uncomplicated,
tell-it-like-it-is 'brother' who never gives up hope.
He is urbane and wordly-wise, a symbol of the new
black man of the cities. Simple is a 'cat' who knows the
score, a man who says, 'I have so many hardships in
this life that it is a wonder I'll live until I die.'

As sophisticated and complex as Langston was, it
is this simple man, a man without education and airs,
who expresses that 'blackness' that Langston strove
all of his life to reveal. The distinguished professor of
English at Spelman College in Atlanta, Donna Akiba

Sullivan Harper, is the author of *Not So Simple: The 'Simple' Stories by Langston Hughes*. Professor Harper shows the complexity of the down-home wisdom of Simple, and by extension of the African American community.

Simple was Langston's device for rendering in the most direct way possible, his own feelings, his own contradictions.

> 'You imply that there is no fun to be had around white folks.'
>
> 'I never had none,' said Simple.
>
> 'You have a color complex.'
>
> 'A colored complexion,' said Simple.
>
> 'I said *complex*, not complexion.'
>
> 'I added the *shun* myself,' said Simple. 'I'm colored, and being around white folks makes me feel *more* colored – since most of them shun Negroes.'

From travelling to Africa and Europe and hanging out with the 'Niggerati' and Zora Neal Hurston in the twenties; to his time in Spain during the Civil War in the thirties, and everything in between, it was Simple who gave him the most joy. Through him, Langston spoke directly to black people and was a success at it. He wrote Simple until 1965, two years before his death. But Simple continues on in anthologies being published every year.

Towards the end of the forties, Langston began releasing pronouncements like: 'The Negro writer has to work especially hard to avoid the appearance of propaganda.' He tried to move his political stance closer to the centre. But it was too late. For years he had been the target of Aimee Semple McPherson and her congregation of fanatics. They saw him as a blasphemer and therefore an enemy of the United States. Her people attacked Langston's poem 'Goodbye Christ'. The FBI began to investigate him. Years beforehand, a black clergyman attacked him over the poem when it was published in a black newspaper. The clergyman also pointed out that Langston had been to the Soviet Union.

The implication was clear.

Ever since 1941, Langston had tried to explain the poem, tried to explain the beliefs that he had held in the thirties and how he had moved on. He had once attacked the second most popular magazine in America, the *Saturday Evening Post* for its conservative stance. And after McPherson's followers singled him out, the magazine published the whole of 'Goodbye Christ' without permission. The poem sparked outrage in middle America. At a hotel where he had gone to give a lecture, a few of McPherson's followers turned up and passed out 500 copies of the poem. One of his readers who had come to hear him speak tried to shake Langston's hand as the poet fled to a waiting car. As the car pulled away, a protestor yelled out: 'Down where I come from, we don't shake hands with niggers.'

McPherson, a woman who had begun her career in her native Canada in high school fighting the theory of evolution, had set her sights on Langston Hughes, one of the most famous writers in America. It gave her great publicity. Even after she was found dead in a hotel room in September 1944, of a suspected overdose, the battle went on without her. Langston Hughes had to be silenced.

Gwendolyn Brooks, the first African American poet to win the Pulitzer Prize, later to become poet laureate of Illinois, had known Langston since she was a teenager in the thirties. No matter what happened, she would say, Langston kept working. He refused to dignify his enemies by opposing them. He was a Langston, after all.

He had written in 'Color' published in 1943: 'Wear it/Like a banner/For the proud –/Not like a shroud.'

He still had much to say, much to do.

But the weight of the times had descended upon him.

CHAPTER NINE

IN 1947, TOWARDS THE END of a tumultuous decade for him and the world, Langston wrote for *Phylon* magazine a piece that could be considered prescient. He wrote about what he called the 'social poet': 'Poets who write mostly about love, roses and moonlight, sunsets and snow, must lead a very quiet life. Seldom, I imagine, does their poetry get them into difficulties. [...] Some of my earliest poems were social poems in that they were about people's problems – whole groups of people's problems – rather than my own personal difficulties. Sometimes, though, certain aspects of my personal problems happened to be also common to many other people. And certainly, racially speaking, my own problems of adjustment to American life were the same as those of millions of other segregated Negroes. The moon belongs to everybody, but not this American earth of ours. That is perhaps why poems about the moon perturb no one, but poems about color and poverty do perturb many citizens. Social forces pull backwards or forwards, right or left, and social poems get caught in the pulling and hauling ...'*

The crusade against the Left climbed into full gear as the 1950s began. Langston was under increasing pressure, as well as the friends and the people he cared about. A poem that he published in 1925, 'Poem for F.S', is believed to be dedicated to and about a close friend, a sailor by the name of Ferdinand Smith. 'F.S.' was so many things that Langston had wanted to be: a physically fit man with dark skin, a free spirit. F.S had been a sailor and it was he who had encouraged Langston, when they were both young, to set sail and see the world. And he had.

Langston's poem to his friend had many titles and it is written in the direct and deceptively simple way that he believed reflected the soul of his people, and which his critics – black and white – were beginning to say was old-fashioned, crude, one-dimensional:

I love my friend.
He went away from me.
There's nothing more to say.
The poem ends,
Soft as it began –
I loved my friend.

---

* In 'From My Adventures as a Social Poet', first published in *Phylon*, Vol 8, No 3, 3rd Quarter, 1947.

F.S, who had been born in Jamaica in 1893, and had worked as a merchant seaman, had settled in Harlem where he became a political activist, radicalising his fellow seamen. In 1951, F.S. was deported back to Jamaica for alleged communist activities. Langston could not help him. It seemed that a part of his life had come to an end. Langston continued to write to F.S. until his friend died in 1961, but it was not the same as having him in Harlem, listening to his analysis of the world and his dedication to the struggle of working-class black people.

In the 1950s, the assault on the Left had become an overwhelming force and part of the American culture itself. Two groups in the forefront of reshaping literature away from what they considered to be left-wing tendencies, were the New Critics and the New York Intellectuals.

The New York Intellectuals' position was clear: a story like the one depicted in Richard Wright's novel *Native Son*, for instance, a story about black, male, urban anger which had become a bestseller and an iconic work of literature, could not actually exist in reality.

Reality had no 'one' story. And any one story had many points of view.

The New York Intellectuals were a group of writers who had been associated with the Old Left but had drifted away from it throughout the late 1930s. Many had been involved with either the Trotskyite movement (the enemies of the communist dictator Joseph Stalin) or other similar anti-Stalinist groups within communism. As their anti-Stalinism gave way to anti-communism, the New York Intellectuals turned their hostile gaze upon the kind of art that they had previously boosted: naturalism. They considered this kind of writing – which depicted real life in an almost documentary style – as being more about ideology than literature.

Ralph Ellison, one of the black writers Langston knew from the thirties, was their darling. His *Invisible Man* was, for the New York Intellectuals, a work of form above content. It is not, but they thought so, and their praise helped make Ellison into a literary superstar.

The New Critics, on the other hand, were associated with the South. Modernist geniuses like Faulkner and Joyce, with their ornate and beautiful use of words, were their ideals. But for the 'a good read' kind of book buyer, these two writers are very difficult. The New Critics considered that to be a plus. Simple stories and words, direct feeling – all Langston's specialities – were considered manipulative by the New Critics. The New Critics never expressed their opinions in political terms, but they were clearly conservative.

After America began to turn Right following the

death of Franklin Roosevelt in 1945, the literary movement championed by the New Critics and the New York Intellectuals came into its own. Their views began to be noticed and taken seriously. The New Critics were practically fascist, while the New York Intellectuals championed what they called ambivalence – life being about both sides of the issue.

These two groups were brought together by an event.

Ezra Pound, the majestic poet and open fascist who had supported the Italian fascist dictator Benito Mussolini during the war, was announced, in 1948, the winner of a prestigious literary prize. An attack was launched by a writer denouncing Pound. In response the New Critics and the New York Intellectuals joined forces. In the *Partisan Review*, their magazine, they declared that art transcended politics. Anyone who judged art on a political basis was no better than a commissar in Soviet Russia. This artistic juggernaut matched the political forces that were beginning to destroy writers like Langston. He knew it, and he also knew that he would have to find a way to survive what was about to come. Because there was more.

The war and its aftermath, the urban anti-black violence and racial segregation, this and much more combined to create a new black consciousness, a 'New Negro', very different from Langston's idea.

Jazz, whose most wealthy practitioners in the forties were white, was now challenged by a new sound. Bebop, with its furious speed and impatience, expressed the restlessness and anger of the new post-war African American generation. Eventually Langston did engage with bebop and all of the new sounds, but in the beginning, Langston felt that too much of the culture of the new generation glorified criminality, drug-taking, and general negativity. The beauty of black life was missing. He pointed out that 'there are millions of blacks who never murder anyone ... or ... go crazy with race'. He just could not understand what was being expressed. As a result, he fell out of favour with the young and the cool.

Of this new generation which came of age from the late 1940s, the best example and its most incandescent light was the iconic fictionist and essayist James Baldwin. Baldwin best represents the kind of 'love/hate' that the new generation of black writers had for Langston. The difference between them can be summed up by the fact that Langston went to Paris in the mid-twenties, close to the year James Baldwin was born, in a spirit of adventure. James Baldwin went to Paris in the late forties, as he said to me once, 'so that I wouldn't have to kill somebody'.

Baldwin, who from time to time, in order to stake his claim as the new generation, took a kind of pleasure in killing his literary fathers and older brothers like Langston and Richard Wright, would sometimes publish scathing assessments of their work. He was to write scornfully at the end of the fifties in response to one of Langston's jazz poems: "'Hey, pop!/ Re-bop!/ Mop!" conveys much more on Lenox Avenue [Harlem] than it does in this [Langston's] book.'

Langston was bemused and hurt by the attacks against him from the younger generation, but he knew talent when he read it, and no matter what the writer had said about him, he could and did write about those he rated with pride and a kind of paternal concern and pride. He reviewed Baldwin's ground-breaking book of essays *Notes of a Native Son* in the *New York Times*: 'I think that one definition of a great artist might be the creator who projects the biggest dream in terms of the least person. There is something in Cervantes or Shakespeare, Beethoven or Rembrandt or Louis Armstrong that millions can understand. The American native son who signs his name James Baldwin is quite a ways off from fitting such a definition of a great artist in writing, but he is not as far off as many another writer who deals in picture captions of journalese in the hope of capturing and retaining a wide public. James Baldwin writes down to nobody, and he is trying very hard to write up to himself. As an essayist he is thought-provoking, tantalizing, irritating, abusing and amusing. And he uses words as the sea uses waves, to flow and beat, advance and retreat, rise and take a bow in disappearing. In *Notes of a Native Son* James Baldwin surveys in pungent commentary certain phases of the contemporary scene as they relate to the citizenry of the United States, particularly Negroes. Harlem, the protest novel, bigoted religion, the Negro press and the student milieu of Paris are all examined in black and white, with alternate shutters clicking, for hours of reading interest. When the young man who wrote this book comes to a point where he can look at life purely as himself, and for himself, the color of his skin mattering not at all, when, as in his own words, he finds "his birthright as a man no less than his birthright as a black man", America and the world might well have a major contemporary commentator.' *

And this is what James Baldwin understood about Langston: Langston's poetry had come into being at the same time as Ezra Pound's and T.S. Eliot's, two poets whose complex verse could not seem more different from his own. Baldwin wrote, that compared to these two masters, Langston's verse might appear to some to be too simple, even ignorant, 'not the way it ought to be'.

But Langston was mining the same highways and byways of the human heart as Pound and Eliot. Like Eliot, he too was probing Western civilisation and

---

* The *New York Times*, 26 February 1958.

finding it wanting. Langston Hughes' choice was to place this investigation inside the voice of a simple black man/woman. He had the gift, the craft, and the courage to distil the longing of human beings for transcendence into two lines in poems like 'Little Lyric (Of Great Importance)': 'I wish the rent/Was heaven sent'.

The young Lorraine Hansberry, who had begun to be active in politics as well as literature, named her first play *A Raisin in the Sun* after a line from Langston's 'Montage of a Dream Deferred' published in 1951: 'What happens to a dream deferred?/Does it dry up/like a raisin in the sun?'

For this young, middle-class black woman, he was the father of her work, the shaper of her vision.

As Langston's reputation as a speaker-of-truth-to-power began to fade within the African American community as far as younger people were concerned, to his enemies on the Right, Langston was seen as one of the authors of the cultural tsunami overtaking the country, particularly the change that was being handed down from the courts.

Since receiving his law degree in the thirties, the brilliant, young black lawyer, Thurgood Marshall, had wõn court battle after court battle, overthrowing the laws that supported racial segregation. In 1943, as special counsel for the chief black civil rights organisation in the country, the NAACP, Marshall won a case for school integration in New York state; in 1944, he won a case overthrowing the South's doctrine of white supremacy; in 1948, he won the famous Shelley vs Kraemer which allowed black people to live where they wanted; in 1950 he won two graduate-school integration cases; in 1951 he investigated racism in the US Armed Forces in South Korea and Japan.

And then came the jewel in the crown, the case that all of the other cases had been leading up to: the striking down of the decision of the Supreme Court at the end of the nineteenth century in the matter of 'Plessy vs Ferguson', the decision which had paved the way for that cornerstone of segregation: 'separate but equal'.

In 1954, Marshall won, at the Supreme Court, a school segregation case known as 'Brown vs Board of Education'. This case literally changed US history by ruling that segregation was illegal under the Constitution of the United States. The battle for equality both legal and literal was stepped up. Black people demanded to go to the schools that they wanted to go to, live where they wanted to live, work where they wanted to work. And they wanted it now. Direct action replaced litigation. Black groups and their white allies challenged the old customs and practices: the racist state laws. And the struggle was broadcast live on television, straight into any home that could afford one. And everyone tried to afford one.

Like the internet today, television burst open what had been hidden, creating a backlash against Southern ways and customs that most Americans had known nothing about. Television made it all personal, creating a new space in the American home, one which new 'family members' like Lucille Ball and her madcap housewife character 'Lucy Ricardo' could step into and inhabit.

But the anti-communist, anti-Left witch-hunt was televised, too, the hot lights and cameras making the guilty seem innocent and the innocent seem guilty. No one escaped scrutiny, even the nation's sweetheart, Lucy. Lucille Ball who had signed a Communist Party card in her youth, was called to account. But she got off when her husband explained that she was just following her grandfather's lead and anyway, he said, the only thing 'red' (communist) about Lucy was her hair, 'and even that wasn't real'.

But Langston had no escape. Senator Joseph 'Tailgunner Joe' McCarthy, war hero and rabid anti-communist, called Langston to testify before his Senate Committee investigating communist subversion. All of Langston's troubles for the last ten years had finally come to a climax. As far as the black community and the Left in general were concerned, Langston was supposed to refuse McCarthy and go to jail for contempt of the Senate. To them, that was what he was expected to do.

But Langston Hughes had journeyed away from the overt socialism he had embraced twenty years before. His work, the poetry, had moved on, and so had he. He had never sublimated his work to a Party line, and if anyone had read him closely enough, they would have seen that his only concern was that his writing, his poetry moved closer and closer to the world of black people, wherever that world took him. His poetry, shaped by the African American community, in turn, shaped that community, too, and if it had moved on from the socialism of the thirties, Langston was right with it, giving voice to the change, to the shift. Moving with African America was second nature to him, and besides, he had signalled what he was undergoing in the late forties when he had warned black poets to avoid direct politics. Why? Because direct politics might consume the poetry.

In the end, it was the work – not the politics – to which Langston owed his allegiance. His poetic voice and the freedom to exercise it was his true cause. For the sake of that cause, he must continue to write. Josh White, the blues singer for whom he would later write liner notes, and Hazel Scott, the great jazz pianist, had been listed in the magazine *Red Channels*, just as Langston had. Their careers had been affected, but Langston couldn't let that happen to him, to the poetry.

If he had to explain to the Senate committee what 'Goodbye Christ' *meant*; what going to the Soviet

Union and Loyalist Madrid *meant*; what being a member of the American Peace Mobilization and the League of Struggle for Negro Rights *meant*, then he would. He would explain, if he had to, translating the work of the left-wing martyr of the Spanish Civil War, Gabriel García Lorca; why he posed for a photo with Hemingway and Soviet writer Mikhail Soltzov. He would explain his poem 'Letter from Spain' written in 1937, when socialists, and communists, and thousands of foreigners on every spectrum of the Left came together to fight against fascism:

We captured a wounded Moor today.
He was just as dark as me.
I said, Boy, what you been doin' here
Fightin' against the free?

He could not be like the famous actor, the famous white actor, Lionel Stander, who had worked non-stop until his Committee appearance, and after his appearance, could not get proper work for the next twenty years. Stander, when asked if he knew of any subversives, replied: 'I know of a group of fanatics who are desperately trying to undermine the Constitution of the United States by depriving artists and others of Life, Liberty, and the Pursuit of Happiness without due process of law … I can tell names and cite instances and I am one of the first victims of it …

[This is] a group of ex-fascists and America-Firsters and anti-Semites, people who hate everybody including Negroes, minority groups and most likely themselves … These people are engaged in a conspiracy outside all the legal processes to undermine the very fundamental American concepts upon which our entire system of democracy exists …' Of course, Stander was referring to the Committee itself.

Langston knew about Stander's testimony by the time he made his appearance before the Senate but his would have to be different.

He began it with a short tutorial on poetic monologue. He explained that his poem about Christ, for example, was in the voice of a persona, not him. He himself had never been a communist but he had belonged to various organisations, including some which had communist affiliations. He knew that the Committee had found 'questionable' passages in some of his books held in State Department libraries around the world. He knew that they had been or were in the process of being removed.

Langston did not object. His testimony over, he was thanked and excused.

Langston Hughes left that day, in the eyes of many, having repudiated his past, having repudiated himself. Langston did not include the name of Paul Robeson in an anthology he subsequently prepared, alienating his idol and friend, W.E.B. DuBois, severing his last major connection to the Harlem Renaissance. Very few who railed against him – the black writers who shunned him, the white Left who called him a traitor – understood.

His seventeenth-century English poet ancestors, the Quarleses, his grandfather Charles Henry and his great-uncle James Mercer Langston; his beautiful mother, the poor hapless Carrie, his grandmother Mary, even James Nathaniel Hughes, the father who had not only abandoned him but had disinherited him, too, all of them had laid the foundation – the foundation of a poet.

After his testimony, he returned home. To Harlem.

'Dinner Guest: Me'
I know I am
The Negro Problem
Being wined and dined,
Answering the usual questions
That come to white mind
Which seeks demurely
To Probe in polite way
The why and wherewithal
Of darkness U.S.A. –
Wondering how things got this way
In current democratic night,
Murmuring gently
Over fraises du bois,

'I'm so ashamed of being white.'
The lobster is delicious,
The wine divine,
And center of attention
At the damask table, mine.
To be a Problem on Park Avenue at eight
Is not so bad.
Solutions to the Problem,
Of course, wait.

His output continued as prodigious as ever: *I Wonder as I Wander*, a second autobiography was published in 1956; he wrote small poems for the captions of a series of photos of Harlem life called *Sweet Flypaper of Life: 1950s Harlem in Black & White* published in 1955, photos which showed the kinds of people he loved: direct, uncomplicated. He had a gospel musical produced in 1958, *Tambourines to Glory*, which contained lines ridiculing his nemesis, Aimee Semple McPherson; he collaborated with the jazz colossus Charles Mingus; he produced the words for a children's book called *The First Book of the West Indies* in 1956, and four years later *The First Book of Africa*; he wrote a daring and beautiful poem called 'Café 3A.M.' about gay-bashing; and there was always Simple, still a huge hit. Doctoral theses were being written about his work. And he continued his friendship with Lorraine Hansberry, who would die far too young.

In 1959, he published *Selected Poems*. He did not include his most controversial work.

The 1960s dawned with a series of rent strikes in his beloved Harlem. The non-violent stance of the Southern branch of the Civil Rights Movement never really arrived there. Dr King was deeply respected in the North. But Harlemites were involved with the Northern battle against segregated urban housing (King once called my hometown of Chicago the most segregated city in the US because of its racist housing laws), as well as the struggle to make their streets safer, create better schools and decent jobs. Non-violence was not considered a useful strategy to attain justice and equality. And to the young, sit-ins and marches were just plain old-fashioned. They saw the non-violence option being manipulated by trickery, the same kind of trickery that had stopped black advancement after the Civil War. For example, a county in Virginia closed its schools, claiming that it needed time to desegregate. Its white students then went to white-only academies which were exempt from the Supreme Court ruling, in other words, they were not obliged to de-segregate. Meanwhile Virginia took its time with 'compliance'.

Young people created 'Black Power' because they no longer wanted to cooperate with white people to get justice. Young poets like Amiri Baraka, who had renounced his 'slave' name of Leroi Jones, turned to writing bitter and edgily brilliant poetry that veered to the dark side. Langston, as he had done in the fifties with James Baldwin's generation, urged young black writers to hold on to the dignity, to the beauty of black people.

We did not listen to him.

But Langston was always available, always there for those who needed his guidance and wisdom and blessing. He never turned his back on the young, even when he did not understand us or approve of what we wrote. The Pulitzer Prize-winning writer and poet, Alice Walker, has done more than most to carry on Langston's legacy and spirit. She met him in the sixties through her professor at university who saw her talent as a poet. Langston enthusiastically encouraged her.

But the times were leaving him behind.

Although he was hailed as a figure of historic importance at the First World Festival of Negro Arts in Dakar in 1966, and had published a book-length poem 'Ask Your Mama', he had to move his 'Simple' stories to the *New York Post* after leaving the *Defender* – one of the nation's top African American papers as it continues to be today – because some of its readers thought he was behind the times.

His *Jericho-Jim Crow* opened in 1964. It was highly acclaimed because the play was written in the then radically new urban contemporary gospel style.

Langston was still relevant, still a game-changer. In the midst of the turmoil and upheaval of the sixties, he remained true to the young boy he had been, the boy who had crossed the Mississippi and dreamt of ancient rivers.

One of the young African American writers Langston helped wrote of him at that time: 'Langston set a tone, a standard of brotherhood and friendship and cooperation, for all of us to follow. You never got from him, "I am *the* Negro writer", but only 'I am *a* Negro writer'. He never stopped thinking about the rest of us.'

Langston Hughes died on 22 May 1967 at the New York Polyclinic Hospital in Manhattan, probably from an infection following an operation for cancer. Always essentially a loner, he died alone. He had written in his will that at his memorial service, Duke Ellington's 'Do Nothing Till You Hear from Me' be played. And it was.

As befitting a man called the 'poet laureate of the Negro', his ashes were laid to rest beneath an African cosmogram – a symbol for the universe – in the foyer leading to the auditorium of the Schomburg Center for Research in Black Culture in Harlem. The inscription in the centre of the cosmogram is from that masterpiece of his youth: 'The Negro Speaks of Rivers': *My soul has grown deep like rivers.*

Now, the second life of the poet – of Langston Hughes – had begun.

EPILOGUE

IT CANNOT BE SAID ENOUGH that Langston's art is rooted in his people. To not understand this is to understand nothing about his choice of subject matter, his style.

The work and life of Langston Hughes is about being a coloured person/negro/Negro/black/Black/African American person of African descent in the West/ African in Africa/African Caribbean/Black British/ mixed race/bi-ethnic/tri-ethnic /human being/ living in the world in themselves and of themselves.

He loves the different colours of black skin, the down-to-earth nature of black people which he insisted on celebrating in his work. In his first novel, *Not Without Laughter*, which won him a major literary prize, he does not write about the glitz of Harlem, but the flat, dry prairie lands of rural Kansas. The people in this novel have skin the shade of autumn leaves, maple sugar, blackberries, and sealskin. And the most beautiful part about this is that these are the colours of the very earth, the vegetation, and the animal life that filled the lives of the people in the novel. This is not a simple literary device. This is what Langston sees. This is what Langston loves.

The late Hoyt W. Fuller, the celebrated African American author, journalist and critic stated that the key to Langston Hughes '... was his deceptive and profound simplicity. Profound because it was both willed and ineffable, because some intuitive sense even at the beginning of his adulthood taught him that humanity was of the essence and that it existed undiminished in all shapes, sizes, colours and conditions. Violations of that humanity offended his unshakable conviction that mankind is possessed of the divinity of God.'

In his supreme creation of the ordinary man, Jesse B. 'Simple' Semple, Langston gives us the voice of the 'brother on the corner', the man who knows the truth and speaks it. In 'Semple For President', a story about Simple's desire to be President of the United States so that he can erase the racist Southern states and give what's left to the dogs, Langston demonstrates his ability to give us the mind of a black man not interested in what white society thinks about him. Langston also demonstrates an uncanny gift for predicting the future. Simple says: 'What is this the big shots are sayin' about us Negroes bein' cool because there might be a Negro President in the year 2011 in the USA? I want to run for President NOW! Because in the year 2011, I will be *too* cool ...'

In other words, Langston believed so strongly in black people, that we would have made so much progress, that by the year 2011 – some forty or fifty years in the future from when he had written the story – a black President would be nothing special at all!

Langston could make these kinds of predictions because he always remained an artist. He held on to art, demonstrating that the artist can be an activist, a warrior for justice, even a soothsayer through the art. To say that he was trying to simply save his career when he appeared before McCarthy is to not understand the extent to which *his* people were his career, and to be separated from them, either by ideology or his own hunger to write, was untenable.

When I came of age in the 1960s in America, Langston was no longer in fashion. We young people were the children of the angry servicemen and women who had returned from World War II. My generation had seen the Civil Rights struggle on television, watched young people our own age being abused by white people who would not let them take their lawful place at school. There were uprisings in our own communities, we took to the streets, our music and fashion was the opposite of what our parents liked. What could Langston's work say to us?

In the decades after his death, my generation has

come to understand the genius of Langston Hughes and what we have lost in not appreciating him when we were young and he was still alive. Even Amiri Baraka, now says that even though Langston's cooperation with McCarthy meant that he had been 'momentarily copping out, it's true ... it doesn't detract from my love for him. Langston for me was the guidepost. We stand on Langston's shoulders.'*

Each generation since has embraced Langston, made him their own.

The poem 'In The Event of My Demise' by the late poet/rapper Tupac Shakur and Langston's 'Night Funeral in Harlem' have a beautiful convergence. Both poets, writing decades apart, tell the same story, show the same depth of emotion, have the same clear eye and the same ability to render all of this to us who cannot always see, who cannot always feel, who cannot always say.

Here is Tupac's 'In The Event of My Demise':

I will die before my time
Because I feel the shadow's depth

And Langston in 'Night Funeral in Harlem':

That boy that they was mournin'
Was so dear, so dear

---

* From 'For a Poet, Centennial Appreciation'. *New York Times*, 14 February 2002.

It is as if Langston and Tupac are speaking to one another. It is as if Tupac is telling Langston what will become of him, and after that destiny is fulfilled, Langston watches Tupac's funeral procession and remembers the young man's words. It is clear to me that Tupac loved and honoured Langston's work. He understood.

In *Black Misery*, a book of drawings – the last that he prepared before his death – the ironic and droll captions that Langston contributed sum up the truth about being black and living isolated in the ghetto not knowing anything about the larger world beyond its borders: 'Black misery is when you go to the department store before Christmas and find out that Santa is a white man.'

And Langston continues to be controversial.

US Senator John Kerry, while running for President during the 2004 American Presidential campaign, quoted from 'Let America Be America'. Some critics condemned Langston's poem as 'the work of an obvious communist sympathiser'. His critics still hurl that charge at him, even to the grave.

Every year brings more studies and analyses and books and celebration. Langston Hughes simply grows bigger as time goes on. He has a second life.

Here is the proof:

The Langston Hughes Society, is the first national body devoted exclusively to the work of an African

American writer. In 1979, the Langston Hughes Middle School was created in Reston, Virginia; in 1981, his residence at 20 East 127th Street in Harlem, New York, was given landmark status by the New York City Preservation Commission; his road, right off East 127th Street is now Langston Hughes Place. (Quite an honour for a man who wrote that his childhood was about sleeping in '10,000 beds'.)

On 1 February 2002, the centenary of Langston's birth, the United States Postal Service added the image of Langston Hughes to its Black Heritage series of postage stamps, and that same year Langston was added to a list of 100 Greatest African Americans.

The Beinecke Rare Book and Manuscript Library at Yale University holds the Langston Hughes papers and the Langston Hughes Collection. The Beinecke contains letters, manuscripts, personal items, photographs, clippings, artworks and objects, all of these about or by Langston. The Langston Hughes Memorial Library is on the campus of his old school, Lincoln University. The James Weldon Johnson Collection at Yale University has some of Langston's work, too.

Scholars revere his writing, but he is respected by other kinds of writers as well. There are some who claim him as a progenitor of today's rap and hip-hop culture: 'The very people that he documented so well, because he was a documentary poet, were the people who created hip-hop,' said Kevin Powell, an essayist and a founding staff member of *Vibe* magazine. 'I think he would see blues, jazz, bebop and this new thing as all part of the African experience in this country. We're still asking the same questions that Langston Hughes was asking when he was dying in 1967.'

Langston would have loved that tribute.

John Sentamu, Archbishop of York, the second highest-ranked clergyman in the hierarchy of the Church of England, quoted Langston at a Black History Month celebration not long ago: 'Someday, someone's going to stand up for me, and sing about me and write about me – black and beautiful. It'll be me I reckon, yeah, it'll be me.'

My own link with Langston involves the great jazz singer Bricktop. In the twenties, she went to Paris, like many young black Americans, to express her art and live her life. She got a job in a nightclub there, frightened to death of singing in front of all those sophisticated Parisians. The busboy – the man who cleared the tables – was, like her, African American. Like Bricktop, he, too, was young and trying out life far from home. That busboy was Langston Hughes. He saw Bricktop hiding in the shadows. He said to her, 'Just be yourself.' She took his advice and became the toast of Paris.

Fifty years later, I was working in the cloakroom of a fancy supper club in Chicago, trying to earn money to pay my university fees. I, too, was away from my neighbourhood in the black community, trying to make my way. Bricktop was the headliner at the club. She was an old lady by then. She had to be helped up and down stairs. But when she sang, the years fell away. I was a bit intimidated by the white upper-class people who were the club's customers. I hid in the cloakroom until Bricktop told me to come out of the shadows, let people see that there was a human being back there handing them their coats. 'Just be yourself,' she said.

I remember this not only because of the great woman who told me, but also because it was Langston speaking to me, too.

Langston Hughes wrote over three dozen books including two novels, three collections of short stories, four volumes of 'editorial' and 'documentary' fiction. He wrote plays, children's poetry, musicals and operas, three autobiographies, a dozen radio and television scripts and many more magazine articles. In addition to this, he edited seven anthologies.

Langston challenges us to live authentically.

To be ourselves.

And to love ourselves and each other.

Heroes, particularly those of colour, are not supposed to have contradictions. The life has to be one long march, cloaked in clarity and light. We cannot accept in them the shadows, the u-turns, the sheer humanity that makes itself evident time and time again.

Langston Hughes steered no one's course but his own and to many invested in knowing him in only one way, that course often seemed contradictory. But Langston was above all a poet and in living that life, contradiction became for him a seedbed and a propellant. He never accepted the course laid out for him as an African American man in racist America, nor did he accept from African Americans any definition of life as strife-riven without redemption; as brutal without grace. He knew what guided him: the legacy of his great family; the mentors he never knew like the great nineteenth-century writers Guy de Maupassant and Walt Whitman; but above all the anonymous voice of the anonymous person of African descent all over the world, and in all time.

He is timeless.

In 1932, he included a beautiful poem in a collection called *The Dream Keeper*.

The Dream Keeper is for children, and yet it taps into an ancient wisdom, one that all children carry as part of their human heritage. When they are allowed to dig down deep enough to find it. It contradicts the notion that the very young cannot look backward, into the mists of time, even as they face life opening up before them. He challenges the young to remember that which they may not yet even know. The best of his work exists at that juncture – where we understand, even when we do not know.

'As I Grew Older'

It was a long time ago.
I have almost forgotten my dream.
But it was there then,
In front of me,
Bright like a sun–
My dream.
And then the wall rose,
Rose slowly,
Slowly,
Between me and my dream.
Rose until it touched the sky–
The wall.
Shadow.
I am black.
I lie down in the shadow.
No longer the light of my dream before me,
Above me.
Only the thick wall.
Only the shadow.
My hands!
My dark hands!
Break through the wall!
Find my dream!
Help me to shatter this darkness,
To smash this night,
To break this shadow
Into a thousand lights of sun,

Into a thousand whirling dreams
Of sun!

BIOGRAPHICAL NOTES

2 February 1902	James Mercer Langston Hughes born in Joplin, Missouri, the second child of school teacher Carrie (Caroline) Mercer Langston and her husband James Nathaniel Hughes. His mother was a teacher/poet and his father a businessman. They divorce when Langston is a little boy.
1915	Death of his grandmother.
1919	Visits his father in Mexico for the second time.
1921	'The Negro Speaks of Rivers' first published in the *Crisis*.

1923	Works various odd jobs, before serving a brief tenure as a crewman aboard the USS *Malone*, spending six months travelling to West Africa and Europe. In Europe, Hughes left the *Malone* for a temporary stay in Paris.
1924	November: returns to the US to live with his mother in Washington, DC.
1926	'The Negro Artist and the Racial Mountain' published in the *Nation*.
1930	His first novel published: *Not Without Laughter*.
1932	Travels to the Soviet Union.
1934	Published *The Ways of White Folks*.
1940	Publishes his autobiography *The Big Sea*.
1943	Publishes Jesse B. Semple stories.
1953	Appears before the United States Senate Subcommittee.
1959	*Selected Poems* published.
22 May 1967	Dies from complications after surgery at the age of sixty-five.

BIBLIOGRAPHY

Poetry

The Weary Blues, Knopf, 1926
Fine Clothes to the Jew, Knopf, 1927
The Negro Mother and Other Dramatic Recitations,
    1931
Dear Lovely Death, 1931
The Dream Keeper and Other Poems, Knopf, 1932
Scottsboro Limited: Four Poems and a Play, Golden
    Stair Press, 1932
Shakespeare in Harlem, 1942
Freedom's Plow, 1943
Fields of Wonder, 1947
One-Way Ticket, 1949
Montage of a Dream Deferred, 1951
Selected Poems of Langston Hughes, 1958
Ask Your Mama: 12 Moods for Jazz, 1961
The Panther and the Lash: Poems of Our Times, 1967
The Collected Poems of Langston Hughes, 1994

Fiction

Not Without Laughter, 1930
The Ways of White Folks, 1934
Simple Speaks His Mind, 1950
Laughing to Keep from Crying, 1952
Simple Takes a Wife, 1953
Sweet Flypaper of Life, photographs by Roy
  DeCarava, 1955
Simple Stakes a Claim, 1957
Tambourines to Glory (book), 1958
The Best of Simple, 1961
Simple's Uncle Sam, 1965
Something in Common and Other Stories, 1963
Short Stories of Langston Hughes, 1996

Non-Fiction

The Big Sea, 1940
Famous American Negroes, 1954
Marian Anderson: Famous Concert Singer, 1954
I Wonder as I Wander, 1956
A Pictorial History of the Negro in America, with
  Milton Meltzer, 1956
Famous Negro Heroes of America, 1958
Fight for Freedom: The Story of the NAACP, 1962

Major Plays

Mulatto, 1935 (renamed *The Barrier*, an opera, in 1950)
Troubled Island, with William Grant Still, 1936
Little Ham, 1936
Emperor of Haiti, 1936
Don't You Want to be Free?, 1938
Street Scene, contributed lyrics, 1947
Tambourines to Glory, 1956
Simply Heavenly, 1957
Black Nativity, 1961
Five Plays by Langston Hughes, 1963
Jericho-Jim Crow, 1964

Works for Children

Popo and Fifina, with Arna Bontemps, 1932
The First Book of the Negroes, 1952
The First Book of Jazz, 1954
The First Book of Rhythms, 1954
The First Book of the West Indies, 1956
The First Book of Africa, 1964

ACKNOWLEDGMENTS

I WOULD LIKE TO THANK my agent, editor and dear friend Judith Antell for knowing how to work with me, and always being there, and above all my darling husband, David Hutchins, who simply makes it possible.

ALSO BY BLACKAMBER INSPIRATIONS

BARACK OBAMA:
THE MOVEMENT FOR CHANGE
Anthony Painter

Every now and again America confronts its demons, walks away from deep internal division, and strives towards justice.

Barack Obama: The Movement for Change tells the story of a visionary leader who refuses to be limited by America's history and determines instead to change it. His plan for change is the latest expression of a movement for justice: a movement that has swept forward with the collective energy of great leaders like Martin Luther King, Robert Kennedy, Lyndon B. Johnson, Harold Washington, Chicago's first black mayor, and countless others who have bent the 'arc of morality' towards justice.

By looking at the biography of the man, this mixed-race Hawaiian with Kenyan and Kansas parents, a window on America in the twenty-first century is revealed. His life touches and is touched by a sinking community on Chicago's South Side. He challenges the lazy assumptions of American racial discourse. He creates an argument for political change and a different America. He wins a presidential election few thought possible when his formidable campaign was launched.

Barack Obama: The Movement for Change tells a story for our times. It is not the story of a single man. It is the story of a movement and of the people who drove the movement forward. It is a new American story that will cascade down the generations. America has changed and Barack Obama's story tells us how and why and what we can expect.

978-1-906413-23-1

£6.99

BILL MORRIS:
A TRADE UNION MIRACLE
Geoffrey Goodman

Lord Morris of Handsworth OJ is the first black man to rise to the top of any major British institution. When, in 1992, he became general secretary of the Transport and General Workers Union – then the largest trade union in the country – it marked a huge break in the culture of British working-class attitudes towards racial discrimination. The first black immigrant to join the governing board of the Bank of England; the first black immigrant to become president of the Trades Union Congress ... he was, as he says in this book, 'always a first' in this respect.

This is the story of his rise to the top of British public life after arriving in Birmingham in the mid-1950s, aged 16, to join his mother who had come to England a short time earlier. Bill Morris was born and brought up in a small rural village about sixty miles from the Jamaican capital, Kingston. As a child his overwhelming ambition was to become a professional cricketer and play for the West Indies; he has had to put up with what he regards as the lesser honour of sitting on the England and Wales Cricket Board at Lord's. His story is a fascinating account of a unique rise from the shop floor to international status.

Praise for *From Bevan to Blair*:
'What Geoffrey Goodman doesn't know about political journalism didn't happen. This fascinating book takes us through the pass door to the corridors of power' Keith Waterhouse

'Through [the] momentous years in Labour history, indeed British history, Geoffrey Goodman has had a special ringside seat. We all knew he had the best story to tell and here it is. It is a triumph of character as much as journalistic skill' Michael Foot

978-1-906413-42-2

£6.99

NAVI PILLAY:
REALISING HUMAN RIGHTS FOR ALL
Sam Naidu

In September 2008 Navi Pillay was appointed UN High Commissioner for Human Rights.

Pillay, a trailblazer in Human Rights law, was born in 1941 to a humble Indian family in apartheid South Africa. She faced enormous obstacles to her aspirations for further education and a meaningful career. However, in 1967 she was the first black woman in South Africa to set up a law practice, which she used to defend many anti-apartheid activists. She also used her skills to protect the rights of political prisoners and remarkably, in 1973, she succeeded in obtaining legal representation and basic amenities for the inmates of Robben Island. In 1995 when the first democratic government was formed in South Africa, Nelson Mandela nominated Pillay as the first black female judge in the Supreme Court. In the same year she joined the International Criminal Tribunal for Rwanda. Since then Pillay has become one of the world's leading advocates in the field of Human Rights.

No. 64 Navi Pillay
The 100 Most Powerful Women in the World
Forbes magazine, 19 August 2009

'I have heard so much about Navi Pillay and was excited to meet her'
Jane Fonda

'Her extraordinary life' BBC *Woman's Hour*

978-1-906413-45-3
£6.99

CARLOS ACOSTA:
THE RELUCTANT DANCER
Margaret Willis

Carlos Acosta grew up in a cramped apartment in Cuba, knowing poverty, hardship and family tragedies. He roamed the streets barefoot when he should have been in school, stole fruit from neighbours' orchards, and wanted nothing more than to be a footballer like any other young boy. His father, however, fearing for his future, enrolled him in ballet school where he would be disciplined, trained for a career, and fed. It was many years before the young Carlos would accept the strict demands of a pursuit he saw as 'sissy'.

Today Carlos Acosta is one of the world's most stunning classical ballet dancers, admired for his firecracker, yet refined technique, for his riveting acting and for his magnetic presence on stage. He is considered a national treasure in his own country, and a matinee idol to global dance goers. *The Reluctant Dancer* charts the trajectory of this exceptional ballet maverick who has captured the hearts of audiences worldwide.

'One of the most brilliant male ballet dancers in the world today' *Sunday Times*

'There is, without fail, a collective intake of breath when Carlos Acosta leaps on stage' *Evening Standard*

'Acosta, strong and sexy, the ultimate alpha male, offers virile dance of force and finesse' *The Times*

'He comes so close to the footlights, you feel he wants to break their bounds and bring the audience onto the stage' *Daily Telegraph*

978-1-906413-71-2

£6.99

USAIN BOLT:
FAST AS LIGHTNING
Mike Rowbottom

Usain Bolt is the fastest man on the planet – and one of the most popular athletes of all time.

His dramatic world record-breaking feats in the 100 and 200 metres have earned him Olympic and world gold medals in the last couple of years. But what has endeared this young Jamaican above all else in his playful attitude and winning personality.

In the first book about this phenomenal sprinter, Mike Rowbottom looks at the way Bolt's prodigious talent has been shaped from his earliest years by a competitive system in his native Jamaica, which has produced generations of world-class sprinters.

At 15, Bolt was 6ft 5in tall, and the youngest ever world junior champion, having taken the 200 metres title on home territory in Kingston. His course to the top was set – but it was not to be a smooth ride. This book details how injuries and a lack of mental focus hindered his progress until in 2005 Bolt turned to Glen Mills, the man who had coached his idol, Don Quarrie, to Olympic Gold.

'Sport's most sought-after icon' *Daily Telegraph*

'He has a set of gifts that no one else has: an incredibly long stride combined with the ability to execute a race like a shorter sprinter – generating the same explosive power' Michael Johnson

'He runs, he wins, he obliterates another world record. Welcome to the life of Usain Bolt, aka Lightning Bolt, the fastest man who ever lived' *Independent*

978-1-906413-82-8

£6.99